# The Buddha of Suburbia

## Adapted for the stage by Emma Rice, with Hanif Kureishi

## Based on the novel by Hanif Kureishi

*methuen* | drama

LONDON · NEW YORK · OXFORD · NEW DELHI · SYDNEY

METHUEN DRAMA
Bloomsbury Publishing Plc
50 Bedford Square, London, WC1B 3DP, UK
1385 Broadway, New York, NY 10018, USA
29 Earlsfort Terrace, Dublin 2, Ireland

BLOOMSBURY, METHUEN DRAMA and the Methuen
Drama logo are trademarks of Bloomsbury Publishing Plc

First published in Great Britain 2024

A catalogue record for this book is available from the British Library.

A catalog record for this book is available from the Library of Congress.

ISBN: PB: 978-1-3505-1281-8
ePDF: 978-1-3505-1282-5
eBook: 978-1-3505-1283-2

Series: Modern Plays

Typeset by Mark Heslington Ltd, Scarborough, North Yorkshire

To find out more about our authors and books visit
www.bloomsbury.com and sign up for our newsletters.

## 'There Were No Books about People Like Me': Hanif Kureishi on Writing *The Buddha of Suburbia*

All first novels are letters to one's parents, telling them how it was for you, an account of things they didn't understand or didn't want to hear.

It was the late 1980s, and I was in my early thirties, when I began to work on *The Buddha of Suburbia*. The success of *My Beautiful Laundrette* had given me confidence that the writing tone I'd found could be extended into the novel I'd wanted to write as a teenager. I had been no good at school, but always felt more alive than the people around me. I was a horny bookworm, and novels got through to me. I thought I'd do one; I did several.

They were not published. But I did write what became the first chapter of *The Buddha of Suburbia*, as a short story published in the *London Review of Books* in 1987. I believed that was that. Then I kept thinking there was more material. If people were not writing books about people like me, I'd write one myself, spitting out all the painful things, rudely, lightly. Someone said to me, write your pleasure. I did.

Reading the first paragraph of *The Buddha* now, I'm surprised to notice that the hero, Karim Amir, announces his nationality three times. I guess he was insecure. Like David Bowie, he was eager to find an identity, throw it away, and start again next day with another one, brand new.

In 2015, Zadie Smith wrote a lovely introduction. She describes discovering the book at school, which she calls a first for us 'new-breeds'. She says: 'Irresponsibility is an essential element of comic writing.' And Karim, my avatar, who likes both boys and girls in bed, is determinedly wild and rash. But Karim knows something that most people don't: that being a person of colour isn't at all like being white. No white person thinks of themselves as a problem for others, a question, a perplexity. No one asks them where they're really from. White people belong in the world. It's theirs, they own it, and they don't even appreciate it. But they do get defensive when you point it out. Karim understands that being a person of colour means being bullied. Yet while white people might consider themselves superior, it's more original and enjoyable being underneath, laughing up at the poverty of privilege. Karim begins to get that his disadvantage is his advantage. Then he stops caring either way. He's free.

If anyone thanks me for writing *The Buddha* I am always grateful, since I'm reminded of how a few decent people, along with some good stories, once got me out of a bit of a jam, and into a more open world. As I think about my novel today, I wish I were that boy again, free on his bike. But I know he's still in me, funny, hopeful, rarin' to go, always up for it, going somewhere.

*This foreword was originally published in the Guardian on 25 April 2020.*

# Giving Voice to a Community
By Emma Rice

*The Buddha of Suburbia* is a book filled with messy humanity, politics, music, passion and comedy – is it any wonder that I love it?

I have loved this iconic novel for decades now, returning to it both in print and in my mind, time and time again. But what is it about this book that intoxicates so powerfully? I believe that the power of *Buddha* lies not only in the voice it gave to a community that had been hidden from popular gaze when the novel came out in the 1990s but also in its nuanced and challenging response. This story surprises at every turn. Karim is neither victim nor aggressor, he is a participant on every level and is able to slip between social classes, professions, loves and betrayals. He is heartbroken by his dad leaving his mum, but also embraces his new stepmum.

He despises the pretensions of the middle classes, but understands the spiritual pursuit of a career in theatre. He loves Charlie, but ultimately leaves him. Like every other seventeen-year-old on the planet, Karim is conflicted, hungry and desperate to escape. He spoke directly to me.

## Adding Context to My Youth

I was twenty-three when Hanif Kureishi's novel was published. By then, I was a struggling actor in London after a childhood spent in inner-city Nottingham. I had attended an all-girls' comprehensive, deep in the city's red-light district, and had taken more lessons on sex education and peace studies than in maths or grammar. I struggle with both to this day (maths and grammar that is, not sex or peace). My school community was diverse, my classmates' parents came from the West Indies, Eastern Europe and, of course, India. I spent many happy weekends at Indian weddings and, as a rare child who hated sugar, used to come home with my pockets stuffed and sticky with sweetmeats.

My mum would say, 'Just say no!' but she hadn't come face-to-face with an Indian mother at a wedding. I look back now and realise all the things that were wrong with that time. The language, the politics, the aggression and the cultural lack of respect. I now realise that *The Buddha of Suburbia* was a huge part of my real education. Hanif Kureishi gave voice to my classmates and context to my youth. I read it over and over, colouring in my memories differently: understanding, learning and laughing. Yes, laughing. Never forget the importance of laughter in *Buddha*!

*'At the heart of this vibrant and challenging tale is humour that could bring down dictators'*

## Comedy at Its Core

At the heart of this vibrant and challenging tale is humour that could bring down dictators. It is laugh-out-loud funny, rude, brazen and anarchic. This razor-sharp wit is *Buddha*'s secret weapon – mess with it at your peril. Hanif laughs at his hero, Karim, and all of his characters. He celebrates and revels in their faults, he delights as he puts them into the proverbial shit. But with this teasing comes deep, profound and pure love. I am moved to tears in the rehearsal room every day as I have the privilege of working on this pivotal and political piece.

This production has been a joy and a headache. How do I keep all the delicious detail and fit it all into a fun night out?

The proof will be in the final production, so you are the judges – but please know that this adaptation has been a headache I wholly embrace. As I comb through every delightful, gorgeous, furious word, I thank my lucky stars. Over and over again.

**The First Stage Adaptation**

It has been a dream come true to not only work with Hanif but to get to know him and call him a friend. I am walking through my past, present and my dreams in this production, and I pinch myself as I watch friends old and new breathe life into this most wonderful and vital of stories. Thank you all. However, my gratitude wouldn't be complete without thanking Daniel and Tamara for jumping into the naughty, angry, urgent deep end with me in their very first season at the RSC. You rock. You all rock! But let's give it up one last time for Hanif Kureishi and the astonishing, life- and world-changing *The Buddha of Suburbia*. Thank you from the bottom of my teenage, middle-aged and soon-to-be old-aged, raging and loving heart.

## ABOUT THE ROYAL SHAKESPEARE COMPANY

The Shakespeare Memorial Theatre was founded by Charles Flower, a local brewer, and opened in Stratford-upon-Avon in 1879. Since then, the plays of Shakespeare have been performed here, alongside the work of his contemporaries and of current contemporary playwrights. In 1960, the Royal Shakespeare Company as we now know it was formed by Peter Hall and Fordham Flower. The founding principles were threefold: the Company would embrace the freedom and power of Shakespeare's work, train and develop young actors and directors and, crucially, experiment in new ways of making theatre. The RSC quickly became known for exhilarating performances of Shakespeare alongside new masterpieces such as *The Homecoming* and *Old Times* by Harold Pinter. It was a combination that thrilled audiences, and this close and exacting relationship between writers from different eras has become the fuel that powers the creativity of the RSC.

In 1974, The Other Place opened in a tin hut on Waterside under the visionary leadership and artistic directorship of Buzz Goodbody. Determined to explore Shakespeare's plays in intimate proximity to her audience and to make small-scale, radical new work, Buzz revitalised the Company's interrogation of the relationship between the contemporary and classical repertoire. This was followed by the founding of the Swan Theatre in 1986 – a space dedicated to Shakespeare's contemporaries, as well as later plays from the Restoration period, alongside living writers.

In nearly 60 years of producing new plays, we have collaborated with some of the most exciting writers of their generation. These have included: Edward Albee, Howard Barker, Alice Birch, Richard Bean, Edward Bond, Howard Brenton, Marina Carr, Lolita Chakrabarti, Caryl Churchill, Martin Crimp, Can Dündar, David Edgar, Helen Edmundson, James Fenton, Georgia Fitch, Robin French, Juliet Gilkes Romero, Fraser Grace, David Greig, Tanika Gupta, Matt Hartley, Ella Hickson, Kirsty Housley, Dennis Kelly, Hannah Khalil, Anders Lustgarten, Tarell Alvin McCraney, Martin McDonagh, Tom Morton-Smith, Rona Munro, Richard Nelson, Anthony Neilson, Harold Pinter, Phil Porter, Mike Poulton, Mark Ravenhill, Somalia Seaton, Adriano Shaplin, Tom Stoppard, debbie tucker green, Frances Ya-Chu Cowhig, Timberlake Wertenbaker, Peter Whelan and Roy Williams.

The RSC is committed to illuminating the relevance of Shakespeare's plays and the works of his contemporaries for the next generation of audiences and believes that our continued investment in new plays and living writers is a central part of that mission.

Support us and make a difference; for more information visit **www.rsc.org.uk/support**

Season Supporters: Backstage Trust, Miranda Curtis CMG

The RSC Acting Companies are generously supported by The Gatsby Charitable Foundation

New Work at the RSC is generously supported by Hawthornden Foundation and The Drue and H.J. Heinz II Charitable Trust

Supported using public funding by
**ARTS COUNCIL ENGLAND**

# WISE CHILDREN

Wise Children is a theatre company created and led by multi-award-winning director, Emma Rice. Founded in 2018 we are an Arts Council England National Portfolio organisation. From our home in Somerset, we make groundbreaking work with exceptional artists and tour across the UK and internationally.

Our home, The Lucky Chance, is in Frome, Somerset. Originally a 1900s Methodist Church, last year we transformed The Lucky Chance into our creation space and a tiny theatre in which to welcome audiences of all shapes and sizes. The Lucky Chance opened to the public for the very first time in December 2023 with Emma Rice's production of *The Little Matchgirl and Happier Tales*.

## THE SCHOOL

Alongside our shows, we run a unique professional development programme, The School for Wise Children, training a new and more diverse generation of theatre practitioners. Led by Emma and her award-winning collaborators, The School for Wise Children offers workshops, courses and other opportunities for fearless, free-thinking theatre makers and emerging companies. For more information about The School and how to train with Wise Children, head to our website: www.wisechildren.co.uk

## THE CLUB

The Wise Children Club is our community: a growing group of allies who support our work and share ideas and dreams. Right now, as we face uncertain and difficult times, we need the Club more than ever! Club members are our ambassadors – online and in-person. They spread the word, bring new people to our shows, and look for opportunities for Wise Children to grow as a creative force for good! You might also be inspired to know that everyone who works for Wise Children (from those who tread the boards to the Board itself) joins the Club and donates to the company. If you'd like to join us, you can do it at www.wisechildren.co.uk

*The Buddha of Suburbia* was first performed at the Swan Theatre in Stratford-upon-Avon on 18 April 2024, co-produced by the Royal Shakespeare Company and Wise Children.
The cast was as follows:

| | |
|---|---|
| **KARIM** | DEE AHLUWALIA |
| **HAROON** | ANKUR BAHL |
| **CHANGEZ** | RAJ BAJAJ |
| **CHARLIE/SHADWELL** | TOMMY BELSHAW |
| **JEETA/TRACEY/MARLENE** | RINA FATANIA |
| **JAMILA** | NATASHA JAYETILEKE |
| **MARGARET/ELEANOR** | BETTRYS JONES |
| **ENSEMBLE/COVER** | DEVEN MODHA |
| **ANWAR** | SIMON RIVERS |
| **EVA** | LUCY THACKERAY |
| **MATTHEW PYKE** | EWAN WARDROP |

## CREATIVE TEAM

| | |
|---|---|
| FROM THE NOVEL BY | **HANIF KUREISHI** |
| ADAPTED BY | **EMMA RICE with HANIF KUREISHI** |
| DIRECTOR | **EMMA RICE** |
| SET DESIGNER | **RACHANA JADHAV** |
| COSTUME DESIGNER | **VICKI MORTIMER** |
| SOUND & VIDEO DESIGNER | **SIMON BAKER** |
| LIGHTING DESIGNER | **JAI MORJARIA** |
| COMPOSER | **NIRAJ CHAG** |
| CHOREOGRAPHER & INTIMACY COORDINATOR | **ETTA MURFITT** |
| FIGHT DIRECTOR | **KEV McCURDY** |
| CASTING DIRECTOR | **MATTHEW DEWSBURY CDG** |
| COMPANY VOICE WORK | **JEANNETTE NELSON** |
| DIALECT COACH | **GURKIRAN KAUR** |
| ASSOCIATE DIRECTOR | **LAURA KEEFE** |
| ASSOCIATE COSTUME DESIGNER | **HELEN JOHNSON** |
| ASSOCIATE CHOREOGRAPHER | **ANKUR BAHL** |
| PRODUCTION MANAGER | **SAM PATERSON** |
| COSTUME SUPERVISOR | **ZARAH MEHERALI** |
| PROPS SUPERVISOR | **KATRINA STEWART** |
| COMPANY MANAGERS | **SUZANNE BOURKE** |
| | **PIP HOROBIN** |
| STAGE MANAGER | **SUZI BLAKEY** |
| DEPUTY STAGE MANAGER | **SURENEE SOMCHIT** |
| ASSISTANT STAGE MANAGER | **CHLOE JONES** |
| PRODUCER | **BEN TYREMAN** |

*This text may differ slightly from the play as performed.*

# The Buddha of Suburbia

## Characters

**Karim**
**Jamila**
**Changez**
**Eva**
**Jeeta**
**Margaret**
**Haroon**
**Charlie**
**Anwar**
**Jeremy Shadwell**
**Matthew Pyke**
**Eleanor**
**Tracey**
**Marlene**

**Jimmy**
**Headmaster**
**Old Greaser**
**Passer-By**
**Carroty Hair**
**Actor One**
**Actor Two**
**Penny**
**Timothy**
**Drunk**
**Joanna**

## Note on the Text

*This play includes the use of the racial slur 'Paki'. It appears three times in this play and the decision to include it was made by the company. The agreement to include this term is not an endorsement of its usage or the attitudes it represents. Rather, it is employed to accurately depict the brutal historical context of many immigrants', and many descendants of immigrants', experiences in Great Britain during the 1970s. In the future, it should only be included with the expressed consent of the actors involved.*

# Act One

*We are in a 1970s sitting room. Or is it comedy club, a rock venue or a rehearsal room? A young man talks into a mic.*

**Karim**  Hello.

*There is no response.*

I said . . . Hello!

*The audience finally reply.*

**Audience**  Hello!

**Karim**  My name is Karim Amir, and I am an Englishman born and bred. Almost. I am considered to be a funny kind of Englishman, a new breed as it were, having emerged from two old histories. But I don't care – Englishman I am, from the South London suburbs.

It's 3 May 1979. 'Bright Eyes' is Number One in the charts having knocked 'I Will Survive' off its perch a few weeks earlier, rendering its message a little dysfunctional in my opinion. The country teeters as, on one hand, the Village People are being played at family weddings and, on the other, the stinking air hangs heavy as lorry drivers, railway workers, bin men and grave diggers go on strike amid food and fuel shortages. Inflation is at a terrifying high of 13 per cent and the country is bubbling with fear and rage. Conservative spokesman Airey Neave is blown up in the car park of the House of Commons and anti-Nazi protester Blair Peach dies from a head injury probably inflicted by the police – although we'll never really know as the Met decided to stay tight lipped in a desire to protect their own. Another world, eh? Another world.

Where was I? Oh yes! It's 3 May 1979. We have just survived the Winter of Discontent and after a brutal vote of no confidence, it's election day. In a few short hours we will find out if our teetering country is going to stay where it is or tip from left to right? Will we stay like this forever or, like marbles on a manhole cover, find ourselves rolling into a different hole altogether?

The answer to that is for another day. Tonight, dear friends, we aren't thinking about politics. Tonight, we are celebrating my new job.

*An eccentric group of characters start to gather around* **Karim**.

**Family/Friends**   Well done, Karim! Really well done!

*They are dressed up in their best clothes and each carries a suitcase or handbag – or shall we just call it baggage?*

**Karim**   Come in, come in. Welcome! 'The Milky Bars are on me'!

*The family and friends place their baggage on the floor, ready to dance around them.*

Here they are. My family and friends – and all their baggage. They are putting their differences aside, burying their hatchets (along with their sorrows) and coming together for me. To celebrate me. Karim Amir.

*The sitting room is flooded with disco lights and the family break into a dance routine.*

*The music stops and the ensemble freeze, captured in a moment of pure simple joy.* **Karim** *walks around them as if they are exhibits in Madame Tussauds.*

**Karim**   Look at them? All smiles and acceptance.

*He walks and talks us through them like a tour guide.*

This is my best friend, Jamila.

**Jamila**   Hey, Creamy.

**Karim**   This is her husband, Changez.

**Changez**   Looking good, looking good!

**Karim**   Here is Eva, my step-mum.

**Eva**    Kiss, kiss, darling.

**Karim**    And this is my Aunty Jeeta.

**Jeeta**    Ah! Karim!

**Karim**    This is . . .

*He clicks his fingers as he can't remember his name.*

**Margaret**    Jimmy!

**Karim**    Sorry. Jimmy.

**Jimmy**    Alright, Karim.

**Karim**    And this is . . .

*He struggles again.*

**Jamila**    Joanna!

**Karim**    Joanna.

**Joanna**    This is such a beautiful party.

**Karim**    Of course Joanna and Jimmy don't mean much to me but they do to people I care about, so are welcome.

This is Charlie. The love of my life. He's actually dead now, but why let mortality get in the way of a good dance routine?

*The family dance again. Then freeze.*

It wasn't always like this. Smiles don't come easy and these are no different. All sorts of tragedy lurk beneath the polyester. Let's go back. Three years . . . Or is it a lifetime ago? Are you ready? I said, are you ready?

**Audience**    Yes.

**Karim**    1976 here we come.

*They all travel back in time. We race through the sounds of the late Seventies.* **Karim** *stops by his mum,* **Margaret***, who has changed into the drab work clothes she was carrying in her case. We are in* **Karim**'s *childhood home; a world of brown, orange and sadness.*

**Karim** (*to the audience*)　I am seventeen. My family is gloomy, slow and heavy but I am looking for trouble. This is my mum. Margaret Amir.

**Margaret**　Hello, love. Fetch me my tea towel.

**Karim**　Mum always wore an apron with flowers on it and constantly wiped her hands.

*He hands her a tea towel.*

**Margaret**　It's a souvenir from Woburn Abbey!

**Karim**　She's what I would describe as unphysical. I imagine that she considered her body to be an inconvenient object surrounding her, as if she were stranded on an unexplored desert island. Mostly she was timid and compliant . . .

**Margaret** (*snapping angrily*)　Leave me alone, Karim. You've had your fun!

*She whacks him hard with her tea towel.*

**Karim**　But she can get aggressive when provoked.

**Margaret** *starts drying the crockery and* **Karim** *turns his gaze to a middle-aged Indian man.*

**Karim**　This is my dad. Haroon Amir.

**Haroon** *stands proud in his underpants and socks.*

**Karim**　Like lots of Indians, Dad is small. Next to him most Englishmen look like clumsy giraffes. He was a fanatical chest-expander in his youth. In fact, he's as proud of his chest as our next-door neighbours are of their kitchen range.

**Haroon**　Karim, fetch the pink towel!

**Karim** *throws a towel to* **Haroon** *who spreads it on the floor, places his arms beside his head and kicks himself into the air.*

**Karim**　I must practise.

**Karim**    Practise for what?

**Haroon**    They've called me for the damn yoga Olympics! What do you think? I'm practising for my big night!

*He stands on his head, balanced perfectly.*

**Karim** (*to the audience*)    His balls and prick fell forward in his pants.

**Haroon** *breathes energetically.*

**Margaret**    Oh God, Haroon, all the front of you's sticking out like that and everyone can see! (*To* **Karim**.) You encourage him to be like this. At least pull the curtains!

**Karim**    No one's looking, Mum. Unless they're crawling up the drive and peering through a telescope.

**Haroon**    Read to me in a very clear voice from the yoga book.

**Karim** *fetches 'Yoga for Women' and reads.*

**Karim**    'Salamba Sirsasana revives and maintains a spirit of youthfulness; an asset which is beyond price.'

**Haroon**    Very good reading, Karim. Clear. Strong.

**Karim**    Thanks, Dad.

'This position also prevents loss of hair and reduces any tendency to greyness.'

**Haroon** *grunts his impatient approval.*

**Karim**    Think I might become an actor. What do you think, Dad?

**Haroon**    You're going to be a doctor! Keep going.

*He stands up and starts to put his clothes on; a serious black polo-neck sweater, a black imitation-leather jacket and grey Marks and Spencer cords.*

I can't be upside down while you ponder your future.

**Karim**    'Remember to extract from life all the real joy it has to offer.'

**Haroon** Joy! Yes! I already feel much better. Margaret, are you coming to Mrs Kay's tonight?

**Margaret** *shakes her head.*

**Margaret** No.

**Haroon** (*to* **Margaret**) Come on, sweetie. It's a special occasion. She's asked me to speak about Oriental philosophy.

**Margaret** *yawns.* **Haroon** *tries to cuddle her.*

**Haroon** Let's go out together and enjoy ourselves, eh? Mrs Kay has invited us both.

**Margaret** *pushes* **Haroon** *away.*

**Margaret** But it isn't me that Mrs Kay wants to see. She treats me like dog's muck, Haroon. I'm too English. I'm not Indian enough for Eva.

**Haroon** You could wear a sari?

**Margaret** I did that once, I looked like a sausage roll.

**Karim** I'll come!

**Haroon** Then chop-chop. You can't come to Mrs Kay's dressed like that.

**Karim** *changes into turquoise flared trousers, a blue and white flower-patterned see-through shirt, blue suede boots with Cuban heels and a scarlet Indian waistcoat with gold stitching around the edges. He dons a headband to control his shoulder-length frizzy hair.* **Margaret** *looks up from her chores.*

**Margaret** Don't show us up, Karim. You look like Danny La Rue.

**Karim** What's wrong with Danny La Rue?

**Margaret** He gives me the 'eeby jeebies.

**Karim** I like a bit of showbiz.

**Haroon** Come on. Come on. I don't want to be late.

**Karim** (*to the audience*)    I accompanied Dad to Eva Kay's.

**Eva** *appears – a vivid bombshell. She is wearing a multi-coloured kaftan and dances slowly like a hot cat. Her hair is up, down and out. Her eyes dark with kohl. Her feet bare and her toenails painted alternately green and red. She spots* **Karim** *with delight.*

**Eva**    Karim!

**Karim** (*to the audience*)    When Eva turned to me, she was like a human crop-sprayer, pumping out a plume of thick Oriental aroma.

**Eva** *kisses* **Karim** *on the lips. Then, holding him at arm's length as if he were a coat she was about to try on.*

**Eva**    Karim Amir, welcome! Welcome! You are so exotic, so original! It's such a contribution!

**Karim**    Thanks, Mrs Kay. If I'd had more notice, I'd have dressed up.

**Eva**    And with your father's crushing wit, too!

*She turns to* **Haroon** *and smiles.*

**Eva**    Haroon.

**Haroon**    Eva.

*They hold each other's gaze.*

**Karim**    I don't know whether she was the most sophisticated person I had ever met or the most pretentious.

**Eva** *moves to* **Haroon** *and kisses him all over his face and lips.* **Margaret** *appears. She is still drying crockery.*

**Margaret**    Is Mr Kay there?

**Karim**    No sign of Mr Kay, Mum.

**Margaret**    Surprise, surprise.

**Margaret** *disappears and* **Charlie**, *a sultry boy of roughly* **Karim**'s *age, appears in crumpled school shirt and loose tie.*

**Charlie**   Hey, man.

**Karim**   Hey, Charlie.

(*To the audience.*) Charlie is Eva's son. When Charlie walks in, women sigh, teachers bristle and men and boys get erections.

He was in the year above me at sixth form.

*The* **Headmaster** *enters, he wears a black gown.*

**Headmaster**   Vaughan Williams. Fantasia on Greensleeves. Four minutes of perfection which you will be fascinated to know had its original debut in the opera *Sir John in Love* in 1928. Close your eyes, school, and languish in its gentle beauty.

*He sanctimoniously lowers the needle onto a record, but instead of Vaughan Williams, the opening chords of T-Rex's '20th Century Boy' rattle in the speakers.* **Charlie** *starts to bob his head and whisper.*

**Charlie**   Dig it, dig it, man.

*Delighted the class dance along with* **Charlie**.

**Karim** (*to the audience*)   For this, Charlie was caned in front of us all and I loved him more than I had ever loved anybody.

*We are back at* **Eva***'s.*

**Charlie**   Glad to see you, man.

**Karim**   Glad to see you too, Charlie.

*Tibetan music plays as* **Eva** *leads the guests by sitting cross-legged on the floor.*

**Karim**   Where's your dad?

**Charlie**   Having a nervous breakdown. He's gone into a kind of therapy centre where they allow it all to happen.

**Karim** (*to the audience*)    In my family nervous breakdowns were as exotic as New Orleans.

**Eva** (*clapping her hands*)    Can I have your attention please. It is my pleasure and privilege to introduce you all to my good friend Haroon.

*She bows to* **Haroon** *in a Japanese way.*

**Eva**    Haroon, will you show us the Way? Will you show us the Path?

**Karim** (*to the audience*)    Dad couldn't show you the way to Beckenham.

**Haroon**    Things are going to happen to you this evening. Things that may change you a little, or make you want to change; change in order to reach your full potential as human beings. You must not resist. If you resist, it will be like driving a car with the handbrake on.

*The room hangs on his every word and people nod in agreement.*

Please sit with your legs apart. Raise your arms.

Now, breathing out, stretch down to your right foot.

*While the class embarks on some generic, basic yoga,* **Haroon** *removes his shoes, socks, polo neck and vest. He pads around the circle of dreamers. When* **Haroon** *passes* **Eva** *she touches his foot with her hand.*

**Charlie**    Don't you just love Tibetan chanting, Karim?

**Karim** *makes a pained face.*

**Charlie**    I think I've got something that's more your bag upstairs.

**Karim**    Lead the way.

*He follows* **Charlie** *to his attic bedroom.*

**Charlie**    Please remove your watch. In my domain time isn't a factor.

**Karim** *takes off his watch and steps into a world of rock 'n' roll.*

**Charlie** *looks at* **Karim** *tolerantly and rolls a joint.*

**Charlie**  Your father. He's wise. D'you do that meditation stuff every morning as well?

**Karim** *nods unconvincingly.* **Charlie** *hands* **Karim** *the joint. He pulls on it and is so immediately excited and dizzy, he stands up.*

**Karim**  I have to go.

**Charlie**  So soon?

**Karim**  I think I'm stoned.

**Charlie**  On three tokes, little one?

**Karim**  I think the door to the future has opened.

**Charlie**  Go through it, man. Go through it.

**Karim** (*to the audience*)  I decided to shut the door to the future and went to find my dad.

Dad? Dad? Dad!

*He leaves* **Charlie** *and stumbles into the living room where the class still obediently sit, but neither* **Eva** *nor* **Haroon** *are there. He goes into the garden and sees* **Eva** *on a bench. She pulls her kaftan over her head and reveals that she has only one breast. Beneath her hair and flesh is* **Haroon**. *They are having vigorous sex.*

**Haroon**  Oh God, oh my God, oh my God.

**Eva** *slaps her hand over* **Haroon**'s *mouth and bounces, head back, eyes to stars, hair flying.*

*There is a huge explosion when they both come, simultaneously,* **Eva** *loudly,* **Haroon** *muffled by her hand. When* **Eva** *releases her hand from* **Haroon**'s *mouth, he starts to laugh.*

**Karim** (*to the audience*)  I was ok about the sex. But the laughter stuck in my throat. The happy fucker just laughed and laughed.

*He quickly makes his way back through the yoga class and into* **Charlie**'s *room.* **Charlie** *is lying on his back.*

**Charlie**    You're back. Good. Come and lie beside me. Closer.

**Karim** *lies down and takes the joint from him.*

**Charlie**    Now, don't take this badly . . . You've got to wear less.

**Karim**    Wear less?

**Charlie**    Dress. Less. Yes.

*He props himself up on to one elbow and concentrates on* **Karim**.

**Charlie**    Levi's I suggest, with an open-necked shirt, maybe in pink or purple, and a thick brown belt. Forget the headband.

**Karim** *rips off the headband.*

**Charlie**    You see, Karim, you tend to look a bit like a pearly queen.

**Charlie** *lays back and closes his eyes.*

**Karim** *puts his hand on* **Charlie**'s *thigh. No response.* **Charlie**'s *eyes remain closed.* **Karim** *opens* **Charlie**'s *belt and fly and releases his cock.* **Karim** *takes hold.*

**Karim** (*to the audience*)    He twitched! It was a sign! Through this human electricity we understood each other. We both wanted more.

Now, I had squeezed many penises before, at school. It broke up the monotony of learning. But I had never kissed a man.

**Karim** *tries to kiss* **Charlie** *but he avoids it by turning his head to one side.*

*There is a huge explosion as* **Charlie** *ejaculates.*

**Eva** *and* **Haroon** *appear.*

**Eva**    You naughty boys!

**Haroon** *raises his hand to slap* **Karim**.

**Haroon**    I saw you, Karim!

**Karim**    Shut up, Dad!

**Haroon**    My God, you're a bloody pure shitter, a bum banger! My own son – how did it transpire?

**Karim** *imitates the voice that* **Haroon** *had used earlier with the group.*

**Karim**    Relax, Dad. You must not resist. It will be like driving a car with the handbrake on.

**Haroon**    I'll send you to a fucking doctor to have your balls examined!

**Karim**    I saw you, Dad.

**Haroon**    You saw nothing.

**Karim**    At least my mum has two tits.

**Eva** *and* **Charlie** *vanish and* **Haroon** *starts to vomit.* **Karim** *rubs his back as he throws up.*

**Haroon**    I'll never mention tonight again. And nor will you.

**Margaret** *appears in a dressing gown. We are back at* **Karim**'s *house.*

**Margaret**    Why did you bring him home like this?

**Karim**    Where else was I going to take him?

**Margaret**    I was looking out of the window and waiting for you for hours. Why didn't you ring?

**Haroon** *pushes past them both.*

**Margaret**    Look at my life. I could have been an artist you know? I got a place at St Martin's but couldn't take it because I met your father and got pregnant with you.

*There is the sound of* **Haroon** *vomiting again.*

**Margaret**    Make me up a bed, I can't sleep next to that man stinking of sick and puking all night.

**Karim**    I'll never be getting married, ok?

**Margaret**    I don't blame you.

*She curls up on the sofa.*

**Karim** (*to the audience*)    I ran.

*He runs.*

I ran to my Auntie Jeeta and Uncle Anwar's shop, Paradise Stores.

**Auntie Jeeta** *appears in Paradise Stores. It is gloomy and grubby. Several lights aren't working and the vegetables look forlorn.*

**Jeeta**    Hello, Karim!

**Karim**    Hello Auntie. Who's the prime minister?

**Jeeta**    Bruce Forsyth? Noel Edmonds? How should I know?

**Karim** (*to the audience*)    Their daughter, Jamila, was my best friend. She had a dark moustache which was more impressive than my own.

**Jamila**    Hey, Creamy Jeans!

**Jamila** *pops up.*

**Karim**    That's what she calls me. Jammie –

**Jamila** (*to the audience*)    That's what he calls me.

**Karim**    – and her parents were like an alternative family to me. It was comforting that there was somewhere less intense to go when my own family had me dreaming of running away.

**Jamila**    You don't need comfort, Karim. You need a kick in the balls. If someone spits at you, you practically thank them for not making you chew the moss between the paving stones.

*An **Old Greaser** rides past on a bicycle.*

**Old Greaser** (*as if passing the time of day*)    Eat shit.

**Jamila** *pulls the bastard off his bike and kicks him. He limps off leaving* **Jamila** *and* **Karim** *laughing.*

**Karim**    At the age of thirteen Jamila was reading non-stop – Baudelaire, Colette and all that rude lot.

**Jamila**    I can speak for myself, Creamy!

*She punches him in the balls.*

(*To the audience.*) I got this thing about wanting to be Simone de Beauvoir, which is when me and Creamy started having sex. We did it in bus shelters, bomb-sites and derelict houses.

*She rugby tackles* **Karim** *into a corner and shags him then and there. Two explosions mark the quick end of the frenzied assault.*

**Karim** (*to the audience*)    All I could think about was Charlie.

**Jamila** *looks down at* **Karim** *and laughs.*

**Jamila**    You only have one eyebrow, Creamy. The Romans believed that joined eyebrows were a sign of nobility; the Greeks thought they were a sign of treachery.

**Karim** (*to the audience*)    I learned nothing about sex with Jamila and I lost none of my fear of intimacy. I loved and feared her in equal measure.

**Jamila** *pulls him off balance, shags him again and there are two more explosive puffs.* **Karim** *pulls himself together and returns to the audience and the job in hand.*

**Karim**    After the night I'd had, I needed comfort. That was why I had decided to visit my Auntie Jeeta and Uncle Anwar.

*We return to Paradise Stores and pick up the scene where we left off.*

**Jeeta**    Here's a samosa. Kalo. Fire eater. Extra hot for naughty boys.

**Karim**    Thanks, Auntie. How's your back?

**Jeeta**    Bent like a hairpin with worries.

**Karim**    Why are you worried, Auntie Jeeta, with a thriving business like this?

**Jeeta**    Hey, never mind my mouldy things.

But now you are here, you must make yourself useful. You must stop your uncle going out with his walking stick.

**Karim**    Why?

**Jeeta**    Some thugs came here one day. They threw a pig's head through the shop window as I sat here.

**Karim**    Were you hurt?

**Jeeta**    Blood here and there, Karim. Ya, ya.

**Karim**    What did the police do?

**Jeeta**    They said it was the Hindus.

**Karim**    Bollocks.

**Jeeta**    Naughty boy, bad bollock language.

**Karim**    Sorry, Auntie.

**Jeeta**    It made your uncle come very strange. He is roaming the streets every day with his stick, shouting at these white boys, 'Beat me, white boy, if you want to!' Sort him out, Karim. And no more bollock talk.

*She squeezes* **Karim**'s *hand.*

**Karim**    I'll give it a go. Uncle Anwar!

**Uncle Anwar** *appears, wild with anger.*

**Anwar**    You bloody shitty little bastard, Karim. Where the hell have you been?

**Karim** (*to the audience*)    He wasn't always like this.

Dad and Anwar had been next-door neighbours in Bombay and had been best friends from the age of five. In the colourful haze of the spice-soaked air, it was easy to believe in the magic of life.

*Washes of colour take us into a Bollywood flashback of Juhu beach.*

**Haroon**   Anwar!

*There is a sweep of sitar music.*

**Karim**   Dad's father had built a lovely wooden house on Juhu beach and Dad and Anwar would sleep on the veranda and run down to the sea at dawn to swim. At weekends they played cricket, and after school there was tennis on the family court. The servants would be ball-boys.

*There is a Bollywood dance depicting a game of tennis and cricket.*

Dad had had an idyllic childhood and it was only when he came to England that he realised how complicated life actually was. He'd never cooked before, never washed up, never cleaned his own shoes or made a bed. Servants did that.

**Margaret**   Now I'm his bloody servant. (*To* **Karim**.) Got any dirty washing, love?

**Karim**   But, if Mum was irritated by Dad's aristocratic uselessness, she was also proud of his family.

**Margaret**   They were higher than the Churchills, Karim! Imagine that!

**Karim**   If Bombay was so wonderful, why did Dad want to come to England?

**Haroon**   To be educated! Like Gandhi and Jinnah before me. To return to India a qualified lawyer, an English gentleman and an accomplished ballroom dancer!

**Karim**   But Dad had no idea when he set off that he'd never see his mother's face again. I reckon this was the great undiscussed grief of his life.

*Bollywood turns to gritty British naturalism as* **Anwar** *and* **Haroon** *find themselves in London. They put on woolly hats and shiver with disappointment.*

**Karim**    Dad just couldn't concentrate. He'd never worked before and he wasn't going to start now.

**Anwar** (*to the audience*)    Haroon is like a lawyer. He is called to the Bar every day!

**Haroon**    I go to the pub to think, Anwar.

**Anwar**    You go to the pub to drink!

**Karim**    But on Saturdays they went to dances and smooched to Louis Armstrong and Count Basie.

That is where Dad first laid eyes on a pretty working-class girl called Margaret.

**Margaret** (*to the audience*)    I loved my little man from the first moment I saw him. He was sweet and kind and utterly lost-looking, which made me want to make him found-looking.

**Karim**    Anwar was courting a friend of Mum's.

**Anwar** *kisses a young English woman.*

**Haroon**    But Anwar was already married.

**Jeeta** *Mere saath shadhi khi ti*!

**Karim**    To her.

**Anwar**    Jeeta!

**Anwar** *in a panic pushes his English lady aside.*

**Haroon**    A princess whose family came on horseback to their wedding, carrying guns.

**Jeeta** *Bandook ki sath*!

**Karim**    They did.

**Anwar**    Which made me want to head for England.

**Jeeta** *Tum né*!

**Karim**    He did.

**Haroon**    So Princess Jeeta followed Anwar to England.

**Jeeta**    *Mehn né!*

**All**    She did.

**Karim**    Auntie Jeeta looked nothing like a princess and couldn't speak English.

**Jeeta**    *Tum né ticket bhéjné mé itni dér kyun lagadi? Meh intezaar karti karti taras rahi thi tumharé liyé.*

**Karim**    One day Anwar made a serious mistake in the betting shop and won a lot of money. He bought a toy shop in South London which was a miserable failure until Princess Jeeta made him turn it into a grocer's shop.

**Jeeta**    *Sabzi mandee banado.*

**All**    Huh?

**Jeeta**    Turn it into a grocery shop!

**Karim**    Customers flocked. In contrast, Dad was going nowhere. His family cut off his money when they discovered that he was neither a lawyer or a ballroom dancer after all.

**Haroon**    How did they find out?

**All** (*shouting to India*)    He's in the pub!

**Haroon**    Traitors!

**Karim**    He ended up working as a clerk in the civil service for three pounds a week.

**Haroon** *is dressed in a dull grey suit and a briefcase is put in his hand.*

**Karim**    His life, once filled with beaches, was now all packed trains and shitting sons. Once served up with cricket was now choked with frozen pipes and coal fires which needed lighting at seven in the morning. The organisation of love into a suburban two-up-two-down semi-detached in

South London beat him. He was thrashed for being an innocent who'd never had to do anything for himself.

**Haroon**   Is it any wonder I discovered spirituality.

**Jamila** *floors* **Karim** *again and tries to have sex.* **Karim** *pushes her away.*

**Jamila**   What's the matter?

**Karim**   My dad's having an affair. With a woman with one tit. She's called Eva and I saw them at it. On a garden bench.

**Jamila** *laughs uproariously.*

**Karim**   It's fucking serious, Jammie. Mum doesn't deserve to be hurt.

**Jamila**   No, she doesn't. Oh, Creamy, you do get into some stupid situations.

**Karim**   Dad should be able to restrain himself. He needs to think about us, his family.

**Jamila**   Does your dad love Eva?

**Karim**   I think so.

**Jamila**   Well, Creamy, love should have its way, shouldn't it? Don't ya believe in love?

**Karim**   Theoretically.

**Jamila**   Sometimes you can be so bourgeois, Creamy Jeans. Families aren't sacred, especially to Indian men, who talk about nothing else and act otherwise.

*She aggressively drags him to her for sex.*

**Karim**   For God's sake, Jammie!

**Jamila** *keeps grabbing until* **Karim** *snaps.*

**Karim**   What's the matter with you?

**Jamila**   No jokes, alright?

**Karim**   Alright. No jokes.

**Jamila**   It's seriousness squared, Creamy Jeans. Dad wants me to get married.

**Karim**   Married? Poor bloke, that's all I can say!

**Jamila**   I said no jokes.

**Karim**   Go on.

**Jamila**   I've been fixed up with a good Indian boy who wants to come and live in London. Except he isn't a boy. He's thirty.

**Karim**   Oh my God. Thirty?!

**Jamila**   He's demanding an overcoat from Moss Bros., a colour television and the complete works of Arthur Conan Doyle as a dowry.

**Haroon** *chips in.*

**Haroon**   Conan bloody Doyle? What normal Indian man would want such a thing?

**Jamila**   So, it's decided.

**Jeeta**   Soon you'll be very happy. We're both very glad for you, Jamila.

**Karim**   What did you say? What are you going to do?

**Jamila**   Creamy, I can't do anything.

**Karim**   Why not?

**Jamila**   It's Mum. With him. I can't leave her alone with him.

**Karim**   Why?

**Jamila**   Because he'll take it out on her.

**Karim**   What do you mean?

**Jamila**   What do you think I mean?

**Karim**    Uncle Anwar hits Auntie Jeeta?

**Jamila** *does a slow clap.*

**Jamila**    You got there in the end, Creamy.

**Karim**    Fuck. I mean fuck.

**Jamila**    Don't panic, he's stopped for now. He stopped when I told him that I'd cut off his balls with a carving knife if he did it again. But it's still not safe. I can't leave her alone with him.

**Karim**    This is so wrong. He can't make either of you do anything you don't want to do.

**Jamila**    You'd think.

**Jamila**    There's something I haven't told you. Have you got your samosas?

**Karim** *holds up the bag.*

Bring them upstairs, will you, Karim?

**Jeeta** *appears*

**Jeeta**    No, Jamila, don't take him up there!

**Karim**    What's wrong, Auntie Jeeta?

**Jamila**    Come on. Follow me.

**Jeeta**    Jamila, Jamila!

**Karim** *follows* **Jamila** *up the stairs.* **Jeeta** *follows behind.*

**Karim** (*to the audience*)    I smelled feet and arseholes and farts swirling together.

*Upstairs,* **Anwar** *is lying on the bed. He is unshaven.* **Anwar** *stares at the samosas as though they were instruments of torture.* **Karim** *tries to eat one speedily as if to get rid of it.*

**Karim**    Why didn't you tell me he's sick?

**Jamila**    Because he's not.

**Karim**   Hello, Uncle Anwar. How are you, boss?

**Anwar**   Take that damn samosa out of my nose, and take that damn girl with you.

**Jeeta**   You have to stop all this, Anwar.

**Jamila**   She's right, Dad. This has to stop.

**Anwar**   You're not my daughter. I don't know who you are.

**Jamila**   For all our sakes, please stop it!

**Jeeta**   Here's Karim. He loves you –

**Karim**   I do! I do!

**Jamila**   He's brought you a lovely, tasty samosa!

**Anwar**   Why is he eating it himself, then?

**Jamila** *snatches the samosa and waves it in front of her father.*

**Karim**   Could someone tell me what's going on?

**Jamila**   Look at him, Karim, he hasn't eaten or drunk anything for eight days!

**Jeeta**   Eight days!

**Jamila**   He'll die, Karim, won't he, if he doesn't eat anything!

**Karim**   Yes. You'll definitely cop it, boss, if you don't eat your grub.

**Anwar**   I won't eat. I will die. If Gandhi could shove out the English from India by not eating, I can get my family to obey me by exactly the same.

**Karim**   What do you want her to do?

**Anwar**   To marry the boy I have selected with my brother.

**Karim**   But it's old-fashioned, Uncle, out of date. No one does that kind of thing now. They just marry the person they're into, if they bother to get married at all.

**Anwar**    That is not our way, boy. She must do what I say or I will die. She will kill me.

**Jamila** *starts to punch the bed.*

**Jamila**    This is so stupid! What a waste of time and life!

**Jeeta** *wails in distress.* **Karim** *leaves the two wild women and goes outside.*

**Karim** *sees* **Haroon** *go into a phone box. He's clearly never used one before. He puts on his glasses and reads the instructions several times before putting a pile of coins on top of the box and dialling.* **Eva** *answers.*

**Eva**    Beckenham 6811.

**Haroon**    Eva.

**Eva**    Haroon. I've been desperate to hear your voice.

**Haroon**    And I, yours.

**Eva**    When will I see you?

**Haroon**    Margaret will notice if I am out again.

**Eva**    For God's sake.

**Haroon**    Don't be cross with me?

**Eva**    I'm not cross with you. I have just had enough sadness to last a lifetime and I will not tolerate any more. I will be happy.

**Haroon**    I want you to be happy, but what you're asking me to do is not easy. Not easy at all.

**Eva**    Do you think I don't know that?

**Haroon**    Things are complicated, Eva. Very, very complicated.

**Eve**    They are simple, Haroon. You have an unhappy marriage and a life that is slowly killing you.

You also have a woman who wants and chooses you.

*Pause.*

Me, Haroon. Me.

**Haroon**   Eva, I don't think I can do this.

**Eva**   You can! You just have to find the courage.

**Haroon**   It would break Margaret's heart.

**Eva**   And what about your heart? What about mine?

**Haroon**   Please don't leave me, Eva.

**Eva**   You aren't giving me a choice, my darling. I will find joy, even if I have to find it with someone else.

**Haroon** *puts the phone down. On leaving the phone box, he sees that* **Karim** *is watching him.*

**Karim**   How's Eva?

**Haroon**   She sends her love.

**Karim**   To me or to you, Dad?

**Haroon**   To you.

**Karim**   Are you in love with her?

**Haroon**   Love?

**Karim**   Yes, in love. For God's sake, Dad, you know what I'm asking.

**Haroon**   She's become close to me. She's someone I can talk to. I like to be with her. We have the same interests, you know that.

**Karim**   That must be nice for you.

**Haroon**   It must be love because it hurts so much.

**Karim**   What are you going to do, Dad? Are you going to leave us for her?

*Confusion, anguish and fear cloud* **Haroon***'s face.*

**Haroon**    I don't know. I'm experiencing things I've never felt before, very strong, potent, overwhelming things.

**Karim**    You mean you never loved Mum?

**Haroon**    When I am not with Eva, I miss her. I talk to her in my mind. She understands many things. I feel that if I am not with her I will be making a great mistake, missing a real opportunity. And there's something else. Something that Eva just told me.

**Karim**    What?

**Haroon**    She is seeing other men.

**Karim**    What sort of men?

**Haroon**    I didn't ask for specifications.

**Karim**    White men in drip-dry shirts?

**Haroon**    I don't know why you dislike drip-dry shirts so much. These things are very convenient for women. I will feel so lost, Karim, if I lose her.

**Karim**    She's trying to blackmail you, Dad.

**Haroon**    Yes, but only because she's unhappy without me. She can't wait for me for years and years. Do you blame her?

**Karim** *is crying.*

**Karim**    Have you told Mum?

**Haroon**    No.

**Karim**    Why not?

**Haroon**    Because I'm frightened. Because I can't bear to look at her as I say the words. Because you will both suffer so much and I would rather suffer myself than have anything happen to you.

**Karim**    So you'll stay? You'll stay at home with me and Mum?

*There is silence, then* **Haroon** *grabs* **Karim** *and kisses him crazily, on the cheeks and nose and forehead and hair.*

**Passer-By**   Get back in yer rickshaw!

**Karim**   Fuck off, dickhead.

**Karim** *pulls himself away from* **Haroon** *and tries to leave.*

**Haroon**   Karim! Please! Please!

**Karim** *stops and turns.*

**Karim**   What, Dad?

**Haroon** (*bewildered*)   Is this the right bus stop?

**Karim** *is devastated.* **Jamila** *appears.*

**Jamila**   He arrives today, Creamy.

**Karim**   Who?

**Jamila**   Changez. My Conan Doyle-loving fiancé.

*We are at the airport.* **Changez** *has two double chins, and not much hair. His stomach rides out before him, with a dark-red stringy knitted jumper stretched over it. He is carrying two rotting cases saved from disintegration by thin string.* **Karim** *holds up a handmade sign with the name 'Changez' on it.* **Anwar** *and* **Jeeta** *join. On seeing the sign,* **Changez** *drops his cases and enthusiastically walks towards the group.*

**Changez**   Elementary, friends and family. The game is afoot!

**Anwar** *comes to greet his new son. He shakes* **Changez**'s *hand and pinches his cheeks.*

**Anwar**   Welcome, welcome, son! Things are really going to change round here with another man about the place. Now, shop needs decorating. You will do. Plus I need someone to carry boxes from the wholesaler. You can run the shop with Jamila and I can take that woman (*he gestures to* **Jeeta**) out somewhere beautiful.

**Karim**    Where beautiful will you take her, Uncle?

**Jeeta**    To the opera?

**Anwar**    No. Indian restaurant my friend owns.

**Jeeta**    Ha!

**Jamila** *glares and* **Jeeta** *broods as* **Anwar** *moves on.* **Karim** *smiles at* **Changez** *who smiles back.*

**Changez**    Perhaps you might take me out to one or two things that I would like to see?

**Karim**    Sure, whatever you like.

**Changez**    I like to watch cricket. Perhaps we could go to Lord's? I have my own binoculars.

**Karim**    Excellent.

**Changez**    And visit bookshops? I hear there are many establishments in the Charing Cross Road.

**Karim**    There are. What do you like to read?

**Changez**    The classics!

**Karim**    You don't mean that Greek shit?

**Changez**    P.G. Wodehouse and Conan Doyle for me! Can you take me to Sherlock Holmes's house in Baker Street?

**Karim**    There's lots of things we can do. And we can take Jamila with us.

**Changez**    That would be much fun.

**Anwar**    Now, Changez –

**Jamila** (*taking* **Karim** *aside*)    So you two pricks are big mates now?

**Anwar**    – you must hide the damaged carrots behind the pretty ones – but try to sneak them into the ladies' bags first. Carrots are more expensive than you think and Paradise Stores cannot afford waste!

**Changez**   I thought it would be much more taxis in England than this.

**Anwar**   But I was speaking about the price of vegetables.

**Changez**   What for? I am mainly a meat-eater.

**Karim** (*to* **Jamila**)   Changez seems alright to me. Likes books. Doesn't seem an overwhelming-sexual-urges type.

**Jamila**   Why don't you marry him, then?

**Karim**   Because you want to marry him.

**Jamila**   I don't 'want' anything but to live my life in peace.

**Karim**   You made your choice, Jammie.

**Changez** (*to* **Jamila**)   Pretty lady, perhaps you could be so kind as to collect my bags please.

**Jamila** *stares at* **Karim** *in disbelief as she goes to collect the bags.*

**Charlie** *appears carrying speakers and amps. We are in a basement music club. He looks in horror at* **Karim**'s *outfit.*

**Charlie**   Are you still fucking wearing that?!

**Karim** (*to the audience*)   Charlie was never interested in me.

**Charlie**   I'm sexy though, aren't I, little one? Like fucking David Bowie.

**Karim**   Charlie was cruel. He extorted not only sex, but love, loyalty, kindness and encouragement.

*He moves a speaker.*

**Charlie**   Not there, you great girl's blouse!

**Karim**   He was a musician. Played in a rock 'n' roll band called –

**Charlie**   Mustn't Grumble.

**Karim** (*to* **Charlie**)   Can I join the band, Charlie?

**Charlie** (*laughing*)   Are you fucking kidding me, little one?

**Karim**   I'm not kidding, Charlie. I think I'd make a great front man. Or actor! Or fucking film star I'm so damn pretty . . .

*He twirls and laughs but* **Charlie** *sneers and walks away.*

**Karim** (*to the audience*)   I had to settle for 'occasional roadie'.

**Karim** *gets to work, coiling cable and shifting cases.*

**Charlie**   Bring me my acid, little one.

**Karim** *leaves what he's doing and goes to find the acid in* **Charlie**'s *jacket which is perfectly within his reach. He hands it to* **Charlie** *who snatches it.*

**Karim**   Here you go.

*He sits next to him expecting to share the pleasure.*

**Charlie**   What are you sitting down for, Karim? Get back to work, you poncy friend of Dorothy. If you spent more time coiling my fucking cables and less time prancing in the mirror we might actually get somewhere. Hurry the fuck up!

**Karim** *is suddenly bitter and cold.*

**Karim**   What's the hurry, Charlie? You're not going anywhere.

**Charlie**   What d'you mean?

**Karim**   To go somewhere you gotta be talented. You got to have it upstairs. You're a looker and everything, I'll concede – But your work don't amaze me, and I need to be amazed. I need to be fucking staggered. And I'm not fucking staggered, Charlie. No where fucking near.

**Charlie** *is momentarily lost for words. Then he shifts.*

**Charlie**   I'm breaking up the band anyway. What you've said isn't relevant. You're not relevant. Not relevant at all.

*He downs a pint and throws the glass away as a band sets up and punters arrive.*

Christ, this is a shit hole.

**Karim**    Be cool, Charlie.

*He examines the crowd with unease.* **Charlie** *drinks more.*

**Charlie**    Be cool? I'm fucking suicidal.

**Karim**    D'you wanna leave?

**Charlie**    Yes. All this noise is making me feel fucking sick.

**Karim**    I don't like the look of it either. Ok, lean on my shoulder and we'll get you out of here.

*A band comes on. The fans start to bounce up and down. They scream and spit at the band until the singer drips with saliva.*

**Carroty Hair**    You fucking slags! You ugly fart-breaths! Fuck off to hell! Fuck off, all you smelly old hippies! Fuck you – fucking all!

**Charlie** *stands straight and alert as if he has had a vision.*

**Charlie**    That's it, that's it, that's fucking it. The Sixties have been given notice tonight. These kids are the fucking future. They have assassinated all hope.

**Karim**    Let's go. This isn't our bag.

**Charlie**    Why not, Karim? Why not, man?

**Karim**    It's just not us.

**Charlie**    What are you saying? We shouldn't keep up?

**Karim**    It would be artificial. We're not from the estates. We haven't been through what they have.

**Charlie** *turns on* **Karim** *with one of his nastiest looks.*

**Charlie**    You're facing in the wrong direction, little one. And don't think you can drag me down with you. I will not end up like you!

**Karim**    What am I that you hate so much?

**Charlie**    I don't hate you. I just don't think about you.

*He rips off his shirt, screams with rage and jumps onstage to join the band, spitting and swearing.* **Karim** *watches, horrified and isolated.*

**Changez** *joins* **Karim**.

**Changez**    Remember. Bookshops, bookshops!

*He smiles at* **Karim**.

**Changez**    And please, call me by my nickname – Bubble.

**Karim**    Bubble?

**Changez**    Bubble. Yes, and yours?

**Karim**    Creamy.

**Changez**    Hello, Creamy.

**Karim**    Hello, Bubble.

**Haroon** *appears*.

**Haroon**    Come with me.

**Karim**    I said I'd be with Changez this evening.

**Haroon**    But I want you to be with me and Eva. And Charlie really wants to see you.

**Karim** (*to the audience*)    Why do I feel like I am being taken prisoner?

**Eva** *opens the door to her house.*

**Eva**    Come in, come in. Kiss, kiss. Go upstairs and get Charlie, Karim. (*She winks.*) Then come down. We have to discuss something important.

*As* **Karim** *leaves,* **Eva** *and* **Haroon** *reach for each other low down, tongues out, pressing against each other. In his attic,* **Charlie** *paces. Now a full-on punk, he picks up possessions and tosses them out of the window.*

**Charlie**   It's ridiculous the way people are appointed to jobs. Surely it should happen at random? People in the street must be approached and told that they are now editor of *The Times* for a month. Or that they are to be judges, or police commissioners, or toilet attendants. It has to be arbitrary.

There are, however, people who should be excluded from high position. These are people who run for buses and put their hands in their pockets to ensure their change doesn't jump out and those who have sun-tans that leave white patches on their arms. These people must be punished.

*He sees* **Karim**.

**Charlie**   Hey, Little One. Come here. We might as well be mates. From what I hear we'll be seeing a lot of each other.

*He holds* **Karim** *fondly.* **Karim** *reaches round and gets a good handful of his arse.* **Charlie** *jumps in surprise,* **Karim** *whips his hand through his legs and gives his beanbag a good tug. He laughs and winces as he throws* **Karim** *across the room.*

**Eva**   You silly, silly boys.

**Haroon**   Boys, I – we have something to tell you. We cling to the past, to the old, because we are afraid. I've been afraid of hurting Eva, of hurting Margaret, and most of all hurting myself. Our lives become stale, they become set. We are afraid of the new, of anything that might make us grow or change. But that is living death, not life, that is –

**Karim**   D'you ever think how boring all this stuff is? It's meaningless, Dad. Hot air. How can you just talk because you like the sound of your own voice and not even think about the people around you?

**Eva**   Please, don't be so rude as to not let your father finish what he's started.

**Charlie**   Right on.

**Haroon**   I've decided I want to be with Eva.

**Karim**   What about us?

**Haroon**   You'll be provided for financially and we'll see each other whenever you like. You love Eva and Charlie. Think of it as if you're gaining a family.

**Karim**   And Mum? Is she gaining a family?

**Haroon**   I'm going to speak to her right now.

*He leaves and* **Karim** *runs to the phone box.* **Margaret** *picks up the phone.*

**Margaret**   Bromley 2431.

**Karim**   Mum. Dad's on his way. He has decided to live with Eva. I'm sorry. I'm so, so sorry.

**Margaret** *packs her bags as* **Haroon** *tries to reason with her. Clothes fly, tears flow and touches are rebuffed. Their faces are full of tears and fear and pain and anger and shouting.* **Margaret** *leaves.*

**Haroon** *looks at his old home.*

**Haroon**   Let's take nothing, eh?

*He goes to* **Eva**.

**Eva**   What are you going to do, Karim?

**Karim**   I don't know. I don't fucking know.

*He picks up the mic.*

**Karim** (*to the audience*)   When I was at school, I got attached to a girl named Helen. She had a massive hairy Alsatian and a massive hairy dad. He told me that he didn't want boys or Pakis coming into his house.

I wondered how many there had actually been. Pakis that is. 'We're with Enoch.' He shouted in my face, breath thick with bacon butty. 'If you put one of your dirty 'ands near my daughter I'll smash it with a 'ammer!' 'Ok,' I said and I imagined his naked hairy back, like Peter Sellers or Sean Connery. I kept a list of actors with hairy backs which I regularly updated.

*There is the sound of a dog growling.*

He set the dog on me, who, instead of treating me like the enemy, seemed to take quite the fancy. He mounted me from behind, clamping his paws tight around my arms to make consent an irrelevant concept. Helen watched from her bedroom window. 'I might need some help down here . . .'

*There is an explosive puff of doggy ecstasy.*

She closed the curtains. She closed the bloody curtains.

*He runs.*

I found myself in Eva's house, a house where curtains and arms were wide open. For a moment, a brief, beautiful moment. I stopped running.

*A bath appears, surrounded by candles and brimming with bubbles.* **Karim** *gets in. He closes his eyes. When he opens them,* **Eva** *is sat beside the bathtub in a kimono holding out a glass of champagne and carrying a book.*

**Karim**   You look happy, Eva. Luminous even.

**Eva**   Thank you for saying that. I haven't been happy for a long time but now I think I'm going to be.

**Karim**   What's the book?

**Eva**   I'm going to read to you because you'll be reading to me in the next few months. You've got a good voice. Your dad said you've mentioned being an actor.

**Karim**   I have.

**Haroon** *pops his head in wearing a matching kimono.*

**Haroon**   It's a good life, and the proportion of work to money is high.

**Eva**   Let's think about that, then. You're beautiful, and the beautiful should be given everything they want.

**Karim**   What about the ugly ones?

**Eva**    The ugly ones?

*She pokes her tongue out.*

It's their fault if they're ugly. They're to be blamed, not pitied.

*She starts to read* The Selfish Giant. *As she does* **Karim** *talks to the audience.*

**Karim**    I thought about the difference between the interesting people and the dull people. The interesting people are the ones you want to be with – their minds unusual. You see things freshly with them and all is not deadness and repetition. Then there are the dull people who aren't interesting, and you don't want to know what they thought of anything. Like Mum. It is the interesting ones, like Eva, who end up in bed with my father.

**Eva** *continues to read as she wonders around the bathroom.* **Margaret** *sits in the vacated seat. She has a sketchbook and starts to draw.*

**Karim**    Are you drawing me, Mum? You used to draw me when I was a kid.

**Margaret** *is lost in her portrait.*

**Margaret**    Sit still, Karim. I can't get your eyes right.

**Karim** (*to the audience*)    For Mum, life was fundamentally hell. You went blind, you got raped, people forgot your birthday, Nixon got elected, your husband fled with a blonde from Beckenham, and then you got old, you couldn't walk and you died.

**Margaret** *hands her sketch to* **Karim**.

**Karim**    Mum. This picture – is of Dad, isn't it? Mum, that's just not anything like my face.

**Margaret**    Well, dear, fathers and sons come to resemble each other, don't they? You both left me, didn't you?

**Karim**   I haven't left you.

**Margaret**   I'm all on my own. No one loves me.

**Karim**   Yes they do.

**Margaret**   No, no one helps me. No one does anything to help me.

**Karim** *gets out of the bath.* **Margaret** *turns her head away as she hands him a towelling robe.*

**Karim**   Mum, I love you. Even if I don't act like it all the time.

**Margaret**   No. You don't.

**Karim** *holds his mother.* **Eva** *cuddles* **Karim** *from behind.*

**Eva**   I have someone you must meet. He's a theatre director and I think he might be able to make your dreams come true.

**Margaret** *leaves as* **Eva** *sprinkles fairy dust over* **Karim** *and theatre director* **Jeremy Shadwell** *appears. He is holding a yellow pair of pants and a jar of shit-brown cream.*

**Shadwell**   Your costume, Mr Mowgli.

**Karim**   Where?

**Shadwell**   Take your robe off, please.

**Karim** (*to the audience*)   I was cast in a production of *The Jungle Book* and it turned out that on stage I would wear a yellow loincloth and brown make-up, so that I resembled a turd in a bikini-bottom.

(*To* **Shadwell**.) Please don't put this on me.

**Shadwell**   Go on. There's a good boy.

**Karim**   Is there a possibility of not being covered in shit for my debut as a professional actor?

**Shadwell**    Did you think Mowgli would be wearing a Saint Laurent suit?

**Karim**    But, Mr Shadwell – Jeremy – I feel wrong in it. I feel that together we're making the world uglier.

**Shadwell**    You'll survive. Oh! And Karim. I think your accent should be an authentic accent.

**Karim**    Authentic?

**Shadwell**    Where was our Mowgli born?

**Karim**    India.

**Shadwell**    Yes. Not Orpington.

**Karim**    No, Jeremy. Please, no.

**Shadwell**    Just try it. You're supposed to be an actor.

**Karim**    Jeremy, help me, I can't do this.

**Shadwell** *shakes his head*.

**Karim**    It's a political matter to me.

**Shadwell**    Karim, this is a talented and expensive group of highly trained actors. Hungry and ready to work. But you, only you, are holding back the entire production. Are you going to make the appropriate concession this experienced director requires from you?

**Actors**    Just do it, mate.

**Karim**    Ok.

**Karim** (*to the audience*)    Naturally, I wanted Mum and Dad to be at the first night, but as they hadn't seen each other since the separation, I didn't think my debut in *The Jungle Book* was the best time for a reunion. So I invited Dad and Eva to press night and Mum came to a preview.

**Margaret** *weeps with pride and kisses* **Karim** *over and over*.

**Margaret**   I thought it would be more amateur. But it was really professional!

**Karim**   Really?

**Margaret**   And fancy seeing all those television actors! I think everyone is going to love it!

**Karim**   I imagined that the praise I received from Mum that night was merely a preview of the steaming sauna of appreciation that I'd receive after opening night.

**Eva, Haroon, Jamila** and **Changez** *appear.*

**Haroon**   Bloody half-cocked business. That bloody fucker Mr Kipling pretending to whitey he knew something about India! And an awful performance by my boy looking like a Black and White Minstrel! How could you do it?

**Eva**   Haroon! You were assured, Karim.

*She leaves, finds* **Shadwell** *and is clearly angry with him. Throughout the next exchange she is seen making gestures with her fists and gesticulating at* **Karim** *as if she were taking* **Shadwell** *to task for something he'd done to him.*

**Changez**   Good entertainment, Creamy. Take me again, eh?

**Karim**   Thanks, Bubble.

**Jamila** *kisses* **Karim** *on the mouth.* **Changez**'s *eyes are on them.*

**Jamila**   You looked wonderful. So innocent and young, showing off your pretty body. But no doubt about it, the play is completely neo-fascist –

**Karim**   Jammie –

**Jamila**   And it was disgusting, the accent and the shit you had smeared over you. You were just pandering to prejudices –

**Karim**   Jammie –

**Jamila** And clichés about Indians. And the accent – (*Mimicking his accent in the play.*) Oh my God, how could you do it? I expect you're ashamed, aren't you?

**Karim** I am, actually.

*He gets back into the bath and starts to wash himself.* **Matthew Pyke** *appears. He is a charismatic middle-aged man. All crumpled linen and thick-rimmed glasses.*

**Pyke** Hi, Karim.

**Karim** Hi.

*He rolls up his sleeves and helps* **Karim** *to wash.*

**Pyke** It's Pyke. Matthew Pyke.

**Karim** I know.

**Pyke** Do you remember when we met?

**Karim** (*to the audience*) Of course I did.

Matthew had come to see *The Jungle Book*. One night, halfway through the run, the box-office manager rang through to backstage and said that the theatre director Matthew Pyke had booked a ticket.

**Actor One** Oh my God! Matthew Pyke! I think I'm going to faint!

**Karim** Who is he?

**Actor Two** Don't you know anything, Karim?

**Actor One** Pyke is the star of the alternative theatre scene.

**Actor Two** He's one of the most original directors around. He started his own company and creates a radical, ravishing production every two years.

**Actor One** Everyone attends his London openings.

**Actor Two** Rock stars, politicians, even the bloody public.

**Karim** So why has he come to see our pissy show?

**Pyke**   One of your fellow actors invited me.

**Actor One**   Hi, Matthew.

**Pyke** *waves coolly at the* **Actors** *who are thrilled.*

**Actor One**   Thanks for coming, Matthew.

**Actor Two**   And thank God someone's doing some classy work in this crumby country, eh?

**Pyke** *looks puzzled.*

**Actor One**   That's you, Matthew.

**Pyke**   Oh yes. Me.

*He helps* **Karim** *out of the bath and towels him dry. He pops him into one of* **Eva's** *kimonos.*

**Pyke**   See you later, guys.

**Actor One** *is crestfallen and watches from the side.*

**Pyke**   Tell me about yourself.

**Karim**   I don't know where to begin

**Pyke**   At the beginning?

**Karim** (*to the audience*)   So I told him everything. How much I resented Dad for what he'd done and how Mum had suffered, and how painful the whole thing had been – though I was only now beginning to feel it.

(*Almost in tears to* **Pyke**.) I'm so fucking angry with Matthew. I'm so fucking furious I feel like I'll explode.

**Pyke**   Might you, in fact, be angry with yourself, Karim?

**Karim**   With myself? Yes. Perhaps it's not really mum who's neglected me. Perhaps it's me who's neglected Mum. Oh God. I don't know why I am telling you all this, Matthew. I'm sorry.

**Pyke**   I think you should be in my next production.

**Karim**    What kind of show will it be?

**Pyke**    I don't know.

**Karim**    What kind of part will it be?

**Pyke**    I'm afraid I can't say.

**Karim**    D'you know what you're doing?

**Pyke**    No.

**Karim**    Well, I don't know if I want to work in that vague kind of way. I'm inexperienced, you know.

**Pyke** (*laughing*)    I think it may revolve around the only subject there is in England. Class. Is that ok for you?

**Karim**    Yes, I think so.

**Pyke** *touches* **Karim** *on the shoulder.*

**Pyke**    Good. We're going to make a great team.

*He leaves and* **Actor One** *jumps on* **Karim**'s *back.*

**Karim**    Get off me.

**Actor One**    Has Pyke offered you a part?

**Karim**    Yes.

**Actor One**    You're a dirty liar!

**Karim** (*shouting*)    I'm not a fucking liar and I'm as sweet and clean as a Body Shop bubble bath. Yes! It's true. He wants me! He wants ME!

(*To the audience.*) And now the world had some tension in it; now it twanged and vibrated with meaning and possibility!

(*Shouting.*) Yes, yes, fucking yes!

**Shadwell**    Yes what? What's going on?

**Karim** (*still on a high*)    Matthew Pyke has offered me a role in his next play.

**Shadwell**   But I thought that you would want to continue our collaboration.

**Karim**   Sorry, Jeremy. I said yes.

**Shadwell**   You're being ungrateful, Karim. You shouldn't just bugger off, you know, it's not right.

**Karim** (*pumped up*)   But Pyke's a big deal. Surely there's a tide in the affairs of men which taken –

**Shadwell**   What tide, you drowning prick? You haven't the experience to deal with Pyke. You've got no idea what a tough fucking bastard he is. He'll crucify you!

**Karim** (*furious*)   Why would he want to crucify me?

**Shadwell**   For fun, you idiot!

**Karim**   I don't care what you say. I can look after myself.

*He lunges at* **Shadwell** *who ducks out of reach.*

**Shadwell**   Ha! We'll fucking see – you little parvenu!

*He grabs* **Karim** *by his kimono but before the fight can escalate,* **Pyke** *pops up.*

**Pyke**   And freeze.

*Everyone does.*

Hold it, hold it. Feel the power. Breathe the energy of the scene . . .

*Everyone does.*

And relax.

*Everyone relaxes.*

Shake it off.

*Everyone does.*

Good work.

*The ensemble chatter and start to take off their costumes.* **Pyke** *addresses the audience, backstage and operation teams.*

Thanks team. Great work. Really good stuff.

**Shadwell**    But, Matthew . . .

**Pyke**    Sorry? Did someone say something?

**Shadwell**    Me, Matthew.

**Pyke**    Are you lost, Jeremy? Shall I show you the way out? You are not welcome here.

**Shadwell** *looks humiliated.*

**Shadwell**    No need.

*He shakes his head slowly and bitterly at* **Karim**. *He mouths 'How could you?' and exits through the auditorium.* **Karim** *looks guiltily at* **Pyke**.

**Pyke** *puts his arm around* **Karim** *and gives him a squeezy shake.*

**Pyke**    Take no notice of him, Karim. You're with me now.

*He laughs.*

And anyway, he couldn't direct air out of a puncture.

*He looks to the audience and smiles.*

I'm in charge now. Let's take a break. Twenty minutes. End of Act One.

*He clicks his fingers and the lights obediently snap to black.*

*Interval.*

## Act Two

*We are in a drama studio. Cool cats in black polo necks stretch and chat intensely. There is humming and jaw shaking.* **Karim** *picks up the mic.*

**Karim** Welcome back. And welcome to 1977, a year strewn with Union Jacks and Jubilee street parties. *Star Wars* crash landed on the silver screen and *Roots* exploded our minds on the small screen. Elvis had left the building followed swiftly by Bing Crosby. The paint had hardly dried on the 'A King Never Dies' graffiti before it was adjusted to read 'A Bing Never Dies'. After Johnny Rotten repeatedly swore on live TV, The Sex Pistols were dropped by their label and Roman Polanski was arrested and charged with unlawful sexual intercourse with a minor, rape by use of drugs, perversion, sodomy and a lewd and lascivious act upon a child under fourteen. Quite the list. To quote Steve Jones, 'You dirty, dirty fucker.'

**Pyke** *enters and claps his hands. The class spring to attention and* **Karim** *finds a corner to hide in.*

**Pyke** Morning all.

**Actors** Good morning, Matthew.

*He looks around.*

**Pyke** What are you doing over there, Karim? It's time to start work.

**Karim** Sure.

*He steps into the circle.*

**Pyke** Everyone. Let me introduce our new accomplice on this theatrical adventure. Welcome, Karim.

**Actors** Hi, Karim.

**Karim** Hello.

**Pyke**   First things first. I am going to have a bit of fun. I am going to write down some predictions and on opening night, I'll read them out. Let's see how magnificently intuitive I am – or perhaps how predictable you all are? Ok?

**Actors** (*giggling awkwardly, titillated*)    Ok!

**Pyke**   Penny, lend me your notebook.

*An earnest actor passes* **Pyke** *her book.*

**Penny**   You can keep it, Matthew. I've got another in my bag.

**Pyke**   Thanks, Penny. Pen anyone?

**Timothy** *hands him a pen.* **Pyke** *writes his predictions down on a scrap of paper and gives it to a member of the audience.*

**Pyke**   Hold onto this for me would you, mate? I'll be back for it later.

(*To the* **Actors**.) Right. Let's get down to work.

*He starts to direct the eager* **Actors**. **Karim** *steps away.*

**Karim** (*to the audience*)   He was a good director – because he liked people. He saw difficult behaviour as a puzzle to be solved. And actors liked him because he gave them space to discover things for themselves. He never got angry or shoved in a direction you didn't want to go; his manipulations were subtle and effective.

**Pyke** (*to the enthralled* **Actors**)   What a strange business acting is. You are trying to convince people that you're someone else, that this is not-me. When in character, playing not-me, you have to be yourself. To make your not-self real you have to steal from your authentic self. A false stroke, a wrong note, anything pretended, and to the audience you are as obvious as a Catholic naked in a mosque. The closer you play to yourself the better. Paradox of paradoxes: to be someone else successfully you must be yourself!

**Karim** (*to the audience*)   This I learnt.

**Pyke**   Good work, gang. Tomorrow, we will start to build our characters. Choose someone you know and start to watch them closely. Got it?

**Actors**   Got it, Matthew. Night.

**Pyke**   Oh, and Karim?

**Karim**   Yes, Matthew?

**Pyke**   We need someone from your own background. Someone black.

**Karim** (*to the audience*)   I didn't know anyone black. I had been at school with a Nigerian called Stanley, but I wouldn't know where to find him.

**Pyke**   Someone in your family perhaps? They'll bring our play a little variety. A bit of colour.

**Karim**   Righto. I've got just the person for you.

**Pyke**   Excellent.

*He sees a young actor,* **Eleanor***, packing up her things.*

**Pyke**   Have you met Eleanor?

*He smiles at* **Eleanor** *who smiles back. He gestures for her to talk to* **Karim***.*

**Eleanor**   Hi there.

**Karim**   Hi. (*To the audience.*) Eleanor was amazing. She extracted the texts of poems from her vagina –

**Eleanor** (*primal scream*)   Ahhhhh!

**Karim**   – before reading them.

**Eleanor**   'Cows' teeth like snowdrops bite the garlic grass.'

**Karim**   Meanwhile a microphone relayed the gurglings of her fanny to the audience.

*We hear the gurglings.*

She was known as –

**Eleanor**    '– the speaking vagina.'

Pleased to meet you, Karim.

**Karim**    Walk you to the tube?

*He and* **Eleanor** *walk together.*

**Karim**    Tell me about yourself.

**Eleanor**    I hate talking about me.

**Karim**    Give it go.

**Eleanor**    Ok. So. My father is American.

**Karim**    I've always wanted to go to America.

**Eleanor**    He owns a bank. Mother is a portrait painter and very well respected in the profession. I went to public school and have seen so many shitting country houses that I would rather stick needles in my eyes than spend time in another one.

*She keeps talking while* **Karim** *talks to the audience.*

I fucking LOVE Italy. And oysters! And Dobermann Pinschers . . . My mother is a friend of the Queen Mother and when she turned up in her Bentley one day, the local kids gathered round the car and cheered.

*As* **Eleanor** *speaks,* **Karim** *talks to the audience.*

**Karim**    I'd never met anyone that posh before. Her voice and language reminded me of Enid Blyton, of nurseries and nannies and a world of total security that I'd thought only existed in books.

**Eleanor**    In fact, I once had to rush away from rehearsals because I needed to make up the numbers for a lunch for the Queen Mother.

*She laughs and* **Karim** *tries to join in with the joke.*

*We are back in the studio.*

**Pyke**　Morning all!

**Actors**　Morning, Matthew.

**Pyke**　Right, let's start the day with a rub.

*The **Actors** massage each other in a circle under **Pyke**'s watchful eyes.*

**Pyke**　Who got fucked last night? Come on! If I wanted sweetness and light I'd have got a job in the sodding Vatican. Who got fucked?

*Several hands are raised and much gasping and giggling ensues.*

Now, release the bad energy. That's it. Shoot it into the air.

*The **Actors** swish the bad energy away from each other and they look at each other alert and ready to work.*

**Pyke**　Karim! What, or should I say who, have you got for me today?

**Karim**　I have brought you my Uncle Anwar.

**Pyke**　Very well. Let's start to find out about Uncle Anwar. Get in the hot seat, Karim.

**Karim** *sits on a chair. The **Actors** sit on the floor like eager five-year-olds.* **Pyke** *controls every aspect of the session.*

**Pyke**　Don't force anything. Just listen to what I ask you.

**Karim**　Righto.

**Pyke**　White noise! I fucking hate white noise. First rule of creating theatre – use words only when absolutely necessary.

**Karim**　Righto.

*Beat.*

**Pyke**　So, Uncle Anwar. Is he your father's brother?

**Karim**   Nearly. They were next-door neighbours in India.
We call everyone Uncle and Aunty. Perhaps I should start
calling you Uncle Matthew?

*He plays to the gallery and the actors giggle. Spurred on he
continues.*

Uncle Anwar behaves as if this life is of no consequence. It is
merely the first of many hundreds to come in which he
might actually enjoy existence. The idea of pleasure has
passed my Uncle Anwar by.

**Pyke**   Shhhh. Too many words. Give in, Karim. Let me take
control.

*He continues to direct while* **Karim** *steps out of the hot seat to talk to
the audience.*

**Karim**   He tugged on my memories and prodded my soul.
He pushed me to reveal secrets I didn't even know I was
keeping. I started to become Anwar, at first full of hope and
humour, and then angry and beaten by life. I did give in and
I did give it up. I told him about Jeeta, Jamila and Changez,
about the hunger strikes and the graffiti. Like magic, I
inhabited Anwar. Under Matthew's expert guidance, for a
few brief and devastating moments, I stood in someone else's
shoes. I stepped out of myself and it felt fucking amazing.

**Pyke** *claps his hands and brushes* **Karim**'s *shoulders as if to rid him
of this powerful possession.*

*The* **Actors** *clap* **Karim** *and he takes a bow.*

**Pyke**   What did we see, team? What did we think? What did
we feel?

**Penny**   I felt pity. Poor man. Poor, poor man.

**Timothy**   Poor man? What about poor Jamila. I felt rage,
Matthew. Pure rage.

**Tracey** *breathes out in frustration.*

**Pyke**   Tracey? You seem perplexed?

**Tracey**    I am perplexed. Very.

**Pyke**    Tell us, Tracey. Share with the group.

**Tracey**    Two things, Karim. Anwar's hunger strike worries me. What you are saying pains me! And I'm not sure that we should show it!

**Karim**    Really?

**Tracey**    Yes. I'm afraid it shows all Indian people –

**Karim**    One old Indian man –

**Tracey**    As being irrational, ridiculous, hysterical, and as being fanatical.

**Karim**    Fanatical?

*He looks to* **Pyke** *for support. He listens carefully.*

It's not a fanatical hunger strike. It's calmly intended blackmail.

**Pyke** *signals for* **Tracey** *to go on.*

**Tracey**    And the arranged marriage. It worries me. Karim, with respect, it worries me.

**Pyke**    Tell us why it worries you.

**Tracey**    How can I even begin . . . Your picture is what white people already think of us. That we're funny, with strange habits and weird customs. To the white man we're already people without humanity, and then you go and have Anwar madly waving his stick at the white boys. You show us as unorganised aggressors. Why do you hate yourself and all Indian people so much Karim? How can you be so reactionary?

**Karim**    This feels like censorship.

**Tracey**    We must protect our culture at this time, Karim. Don't you agree?

**Karim**    No. Truth has a higher value.

**Tracey**    Truth? Who defines it? What truth?

It's white truth you're defending here. It's white truth we're discussing.

**Karim**    Matthew! Tell her that this is my life. I'm not making a political statement or siding with the white man. This is what happened and is still happening. Tell her!

**Pyke**    Karim, I agree with Tracey. You'll have to rethink.

**Karim**    I don't want to. This isn't right.

**Pyke**    Stop fucking arguing and just do what I say, Karim.

**Karim**    Why should I?

**Pyke**    Because I say so.

*There is a tense silence.*

Everybody. Go home. We're done for the day.

*The* **Actors** *pack up their things and leave.* **Tracey** *smugly sucks up to* **Pyke**.

**Tracey**    Night, Matthew.

**Pyke** *and* **Karim** *stare at each other and* **Eleanor** *watches anxiously.*

**Pyke**    Do you have something to say to me, Karim?

**Karim**    You should have backed me.

**Pyke**    I don't have to do anything. I'm the director. I use my judgement to select, edit and craft a piece that has political, personal and emotional integrity.

**Karim**    Integrity? But I am the only one who is bringing integrity to this show.

**Pyke**    And with respect, your integrity wouldn't exist without me. How can I put it? I know. This is my show. I decide. Take him home, Ellie.

**Eleanor**    Come on, Karim. Matthew knows what he is doing.

**Karim**   Does he?

*He picks up the mic and addresses the audience.*

When I was at school I was punched and kicked to the ground by a teacher because I called him a queer after he sat me on his knee and tickled me. I have been affectionately called Shitface and Curryface all my life and am used to being covered in spit and snot and chalk and wood-shavings. We did a lot of woodwork at the school because they didn't think we could deal with books, and the other kids liked to lock me and my friends in the storeroom and chant 'Manchester United, Manchester United, we are the boot boys' as they held chisels to our throats and cut off our shoelaces. One day the woodwork teacher had a heart attack right in front of our eyes as one of the lads put another kid's prick in a vice and started to turn the handle. One kid tried to brand my arm with a red-hot lump of metal because Pakis should be labelled. Someone else pissed over my shoes, and all my Dad thought about was me becoming a doctor. I just considered myself lucky to get home without serious injury. Fuck you, Dad, fuck you, Charles Dickens –

*He turns to* **Pyke**.

**Karim**   – and fuck you, Matthew. Nothing's changed. Is that enough integrity for you?

**Pyke**   This is boring now. Just choose another character. Give the Conan Doyle-loving fiancé a whirl.

*He disappears leaving* **Eleanor** *and* **Karim**. **Karim** *is still raging.*

**Eleanor**   Come on, sweetie. He's only trying to help.

**Karim**   No, he's not. He's putting my prick in a vice.

**Eleanor** *starts to cry.*

**Karim**   What's the matter?

**Eleanor**   Everything, sweet boy. Fucking everything.

**Karim**   What's happened?

**Eleanor**  Nothing's happened. It's just . . . life is so fucking cruel. And complicated.

**Karim**  What can I do?

**Eleanor**  Look after me. I don't like to be alone and I feel safe with you.

**Karim**  I'll do whatever you need.

**Eleanor**  Will you put me to bed? I might actually sleep if you are watching over me.

**Karim**  Or I could hop in beside you and see what happens?

*He cups* **Eleanor***'s breast with his hand which she gently removes.*

**Eleanor**  I don't think we should, not just at the moment, do you?

*He holds her arms out like a child and* **Karim** *holds her as she sobs inconsolably. She sobs as he addresses the audience.*

**Karim**  I started staying over at Eleanor's. I held her as she shook with untold griefs and watched her as she slept. She would look deep into my eyes and touch my cheek with such tender sadness that I felt my own heart would break in sympathy.

I studied Changez (even though he asked me not to) and I offered him up to Pyke. I pushed out my belly and waddled, I turned on the accent and I carried a copy of Sherlock Holmes with me at all times. Matthew was delighted.

*The lights ping on and we are back in the studio.*

**Pyke**  There it is! Yes! We have a show. We have a fucking show. Class, race, fucking and farce. What more could anyone want? Get in! Now, my beauties, go home and feast and fornicate like champions! Leave! Love! Prosper!

*The* **Actors** *applaud him and he takes a bow before waving them away.* **Pyke** *stops* **Karim** *as he is leaving.*

**Pyke**   Hey, Karim. Well done today. I trust you will also be fucking like a champion tonight?

**Karim**   You should know, Matthew, that I'm going out with Eleanor now.

**Pyke**   I know that, Karim.

**Karim**   Yeah?

*He nods.*

**Pyke**   You're good for her. Calming. She was depressed for a long time. Really depressed, Karim. You give her hope.

**Karim** *takes in this information.*

**Karim**   Oh God. I didn't know . . .

**Pyke**   You should also know that I'm very pleased with your contribution to the show. So, in celebration, I've decided to give you a very special present.

**Karim**   I don't need a present, Matthew. I don't think you realise what this job means to me.

**Pyke**   Of course I realise. We're having some people round for supper on Saturday. Bring Eleanor along. It'll be nice to see you both. Away from the space.

**Karim**   Ok. Thanks

**Pyke**   Now, your present.

**Karim**   What is it?

**Pyke**   Not what. Who.

**Karim**   Who? Who is it?

**Pyke**   It's Marlene.

**Karim** (*to the audience*)   His wife's name was Marlene.

**Pyke**   If you want her, she's yours. She wants you.

**Karim**   Me?

**Pyke**   Yes.

**Karim**   She wants me? For what?

*We are at **Pyke**'s house. **Eleanor** and **Karim** stand awkwardly in the lounge.*

**Karim** (*to the audience*)   I'd had a haircut at Sassoon in Sloane Street and my balls, recently talcum-powdered, were as fragrantly dusted and tasty as Turkish Delight.

**Pyke**   Welcome! Make yourselves at home. We'll be down in a minute.

*He takes their coats and they are alone.*

**Eleanor**   Isn't it brilliant that Matthew's asked us over. He doesn't usually hang out with actors, does he?

**Karim**   No.

**Eleanor**   Why us, then?

**Karim**   Because he loves us so much.

**Eleanor**   Well, whatever happens, we mustn't deny each other this experience.

**Karim** (*to the audience*)   She looked at me as if she wanted to press a hard grain of rice down the end of my penis.

(*To **Eleanor**.*) What experience are you talking about, Eleanor?

**Eleanor**   Don't look at me like that.

**Karim**   Like what?

**Eleanor**   Like you want to crush me, Karim.

**Karim**   I don't want to crush you, I want to help you. Why didn't you tell me about your depression?

**Eleanor**   Please don't talk about it, Karim. You have no idea who I am or what I've been through.

**Karim**   That's not a reason to not talk about it.

**Eleanor**   It is to me. I'm not a freak show, Karim. I'm going to the toilet.

**Karim**   Eleanor, why don't we talk about this stuff?

**Eleanor**   Because you don't understand me. It would be dangerous for me to lay myself open to you.

*She leaves.* **Eva** *pops out from behind the drinks cabinet.*

**Eva**   This party is a terrific chance! You must invite Matthew over to mine some time in the next couple of weeks. Ooh! This open-plan is to die for!

**Jamila** *appears from behind the couch.*

**Karim**   Well? What d'you think, Jammie? Should I even be here?

**Jamila**   Oh, I don't know, Creamy. You always do what you want anyway. But if you're asking, I wouldn't want to be anywhere near these people if I were you.

**Karim**   Aren't you curious to find out how the rich and successful live?

**Jamila**   No. I'm worried that they're taking you over, these people. You're moving away from the real world.

**Karim**   What real world? There is no real world, is there?

**Jamila**   Yes, the world of ordinary people and the shit they have to deal with – unemployment, bad housing, boredom. Soon you won't understand anything about the essential stuff.

**Karim**   But, Jammie, they're shit-hot powerful people. Aren't you curious to find out how the rich and successful live?

**Jamila**   I'm less interested in home furnishings than you, dear. And, to be honest, I wouldn't want to be anywhere near these people. Now, when are you coming to see us? I've got a big pot of hot dahl that's going uneaten. I won't even let Changez near it – I'm saving it for you, my old lover.

**Haroon** *pops his head through the window.*

**Haroon**    Eleanor is wonderful!

**Karim**    Dad was so terrified that I might be gay that he was excited by even the suggestion of a girlfriend.

**Haroon**    She's a keeper, Karim.

**Eva**    She really is. Look after her!

**Karim**    Thanks, Eva. Thanks, Jammie. Thanks, Dad.

**Eva**, **Haroon** and **Jamila** *disappear as* **Eleanor**, **Marlene** *and* **Pyke** *reappear.*

**Pyke**    Well, isn't everyone looking and smelling lovely!

**Marlene**    Lovely!

**Pyke**    No need to stand on ceremony.

**Marlene**    Let's get this party started!

*Drinks are poured and glasses raised.*

**Pyke**    To us. To love. To freedom. To sex-ploration!

**Pyke** *and* **Eleanor** *and* **Karim** *and* **Marlene** *slow dance.* **Pyke** *nods at* **Marlene** *then winks at* **Eleanor**. *She follows him into the garden leaving* **Karim** *and* **Marlene** *alone.* **Marlene** *sits beside* **Karim** *and puts her arm around him. He pretends it isn't there.*

**Marlene**    Hello, Karim.

**Karim**    Hello, Marlene. Where have Eleanor and Matthew gone?

**Marlene**    Don't worry about them. You're with me now.

**Karim**    But . . .

**Marlene**    No buts, sexy boy.

**Karim**   Are there more guests arriving? I thought this was going to be a party.

**Marlene**   It is a party, but no more guests. Just you. And me. Here and now.

**Karim**   I think I should go and find Eleanor. She might . . .

**Marlene**   Might what?

**Karim**   Need me?

**Marlene**   She's fine, Karim. Matthew is looking after her. Stop worrying. Live in the present, Karim.

**Karim**   You and me. Here and now. More champagne?

**Marlene**   I'd prefer a kiss?

**Karim**   What?

*He recoils.*

**Marlene**   Do I shock you? It's just a kiss.

**Karim**   I thought you said kid, not kiss.

**Marlene**   Perhaps that later, but now . . .

**Karim**   Ok.

**Marlene**   Ok?

*They kiss.* **Pyke** *and* **Eleanor** *come back in.* **Karim** *sees them as he is flipped around like* **Marlene**'s *rag doll.* **Pyke** *separates from* **Eleanor** *and walks to* **Karim.**

**Karim** (*to the audience*)   His body was carrying his erection in my direction, like a lorry sustaining a crane.

**Pyke**   That looks fun.

**Karim**   Marlene, shall I –

(*To the audience.*) But before I could complete the question, England's most interesting and radical theatre director was inserting his cock between my speaking lips. I could appreciate the privilege, but I didn't like it much. It seemed an imposition. So I gave his dick a South London swipe – not enough to have my part in the play reduced – but enough to give him a jolt.

**Eleanor** *kisses* **Pyke**. *He puts his hand between her legs.* **Marlene** *is transfixed. She moves around for a better look.*

**Marlene**    Oh yes, yes. It's so beautiful, so beautiful, I can't believe it.

**Pyke**    Stop talking, Marlene.

**Marlene**    But I can't believe it, can you, Karim?

**Karim**    It is indeed unbelievable.

**Eleanor** *takes* **Pyke**'s *hand and puts his fingers in* **Karim**'s *mouth.*

**Eleanor**    Don't let me have all the fun.

**Marlene** *nods vigorously.*

**Marlene**    Yes?

**Karim** (*to the audience*)    It was difficult for me to reply with a mouthful of Pyke's fingers, but I suppose the answer was yes.

**Marlene**    Oh yes, yes!

**Pyke**    Calm down, Marlene!

**Marlene**    I am calm.

**Pyke**    Bloody hell, woman!

*He wrestles with* **Marlene** *and they fall back onto the couch, legs akimbo with a howl of pleasure. There is a big explosion.*

*When the smoke clears we are in Paradise Stores.* **Changez** *is sleeping as a shoplifter steals a jar of herrings.* **Anwar** *picks up a bunch of bananas and throws them, hitting* **Changez** *so hard he topples off his stool.* **Jeeta** *checks if he is still alive.*

**Anwar**    You fucking fat useless bastard! What are you doing?

**Karim**   He's recuperating from the banana assault.

**Anwar**   I'll recuperate his fucking balls with a fucking flame-thrower! Perhaps I will phone the National Front and give them Changez's name, eh? What a good idea, eh!

**Karim**   Come on, Changez. Let's get you upstairs.

*He and* **Changez** *make their escape to the upstairs flat where* **Jamila** *is reading at the table.* **Karim** *takes off his jacket and* **Changez** *tries it on with delight.*

**Changez**   You are very daring and non-conformist, yaar. Look how you dress. Like a gypsy vagabond! Why doesn't your father discipline you very hard?

**Karim**   My father's too busy with the woman he ran off with to worry about me.

**Changez**   This whole country has gone sexually insane. Your father should go back home for some years and take you with him.

**Karim** (*to the audience*)   Changez was a kept man. He was supported by Anwar who paid his rent, by Jamila who paid for everything else, by Jeeta who cooked his meals and I even helped him out with money I got from Dad. It was impossible not to feel responsible for such a innocent abroad. Jamila neither liked nor disliked her husband. But late at night the two of them played cards, and she'd ask him about India.

*We see them play cards together.* **Jamila** *continues as if he is still there as* **Changez** *slips away to talk with* **Karim**.

**Changez**   D'you think my Jammie will ever go in bed with me? She is my wife, after all. Please, what is your true and honest estimation of my chances in this respect?

**Karim**   You have no chance.

**Changez**   Why?

**Karim**   You're too ugly for her.

**Changez**    Really?

**Karim**    Your face. Your body. The whole lot. Jamila's a quality person, you know that.

**Changez**    I would like to have children with my wife.

**Karim**    Out of the question.

**Anwar** *appears.*

**Anwar**    Is Jamila expecting yet?

**Changez**    Expecting what?

**Anwar**    My bloody grandson! Surely, surely there must be something between this donkey's legs?

**Changez**    There is more between this donkey's legs than there is between your donkey's ears!

*They fight but* **Jeeta** *breaks them up and takes* **Anwar** *away.*

**Changez**    That bastard, what does he think I am, his servant? I'm going out for air.

**Karim**    Ok, Changez. I love you, man.

**Changez**    I love you too.

*He leaves. Without words,* **Karim** *takes* **Jamila***'s hand and takes her to bed. Entwined they talk.*

**Karim**    Don't you care for him at all?

**Jamila**    He's sweet. The way he grunts with satisfaction as he reads, and bumbles around the place asking me if I want some keema. But I was compelled to marry him. I don't want him here and I don't see why I should care for him as well.

**Karim**    What if he loves you, Jammie?

**Jamila**    Karim, this world is full of people needing sympathy, oppressed people in this racist country, who face violence every day. It is them I sympathise with, not my husband.

**Karim** *covers her in little kisses.*

**Jamila**   But what about you, Karim? You're sad, aren't you?

**Karim**   I suppose I am.

*They make love. Tender, honest love.* **Changez** *returns. Unseen he watches. A soft slow explosion of colour comes from the bed. In the peaceful afterglow,* **Karim** *and* **Changez***'s eyes meet.*

**Karim**   Changez. I . . . I'm . . .

**Changez**   Please. No.

*He turns away.*

**Karim** (*to the audience*)   I'd betrayed everyone. And it got worse. A few days later, Anwar was on his way back from the mosque when he spotted Changez coming out of Catford's largest sex shop, Lounge of Love.

*We see* **Changez** *carrying a large brown paper bag and saying a friendly goodbye to the ladies inside. Enraged,* **Anwar** *lets out a yell, raises his stick and lunges at* **Changez**.

**Anwar**   You dirty fucking bastard!

**Changez** *withdraws a knobbly pink dildo from its paper-bag sheath, and with a Muslim warrior shout whacks* **Anwar** *over the head with it. He falls to the ground like a stone.*

**Karim**   Uncle Anwar, who'd come from India to make his fortune and return home to build a house like my grandfather's on Juhu beach, would never have guessed all those ago that he would be knocked unconscious by a sex-aid. His heart failed, and after a week in intensive care, Anwar died, mumbling about Bombay, about the beach and calling for his mother.

**Jamila**, **Changez** *and* **Karim** *sit on the pavement as* **Jeeta** *cleans the shop behind them. She throws out bags of rubbish as she clears the way for a new start.*

**Jeeta**   Good riddance.

**Jamila**    All of this has made me think about what I want in my life.

**Karim**    What do you want?

**Jamila**    I want to live somewhere else.

**Changez**    Elsewhere where?

**Jamila**    I want to try and live in another way. I feel isolated.

**Changez**    I am there daily.

**Jamila**    Changez, I want to live communally with a bunch of people – friends – in a large house they've bought in Peckham.

*She slides her hand over his as she breaks the news.*

**Karim**    Jammie, you can't. What about Changez?

**Jamila**    Changez, what would you like to do?

**Changez**    Go with you. Go together, eh? Husband and wife, always together, despite our difficult characters, eh?

**Jamila**    No.

**Karim**    He won't be able to survive alone, Jammie. And I'm going on tour soon. What'll happen to him?

**Jamila** (*to* **Changez**)    That's for you to think about. Why don't you go back to your family in Bombay? There are servants, chauffeurs.

**Changez**    But you are my wife.

**Jamila** (*gently*)    Only legally.

**Changez**    The legal is nothing. In my heart you are my Jamila.

**Jamila**    Changez, you know it's never been like that.

**Changez**    I'm not going back. You cannot make me.

**Jamila**    I am not making you do anything. You must do what you need to do. Be where you need to be.

**Changez**    This is too Western for me. No one cares for another in this capitalism of the feelings. Everyone is left to rot alone.

*A fox walks past and finds treasure in one of the bin bags.* **Jeeta** *watches him.*

**Jeeta**    Hello, brother fox. Are you looking for my chicken? My chicken is good. Everybody wants my chicken.

*She has a thought and runs inside.*

**Jamila** (*to* **Changez**)    Would you like to come with me?

**Changez**    Is that possible?

**Jamila**    We won't be husband and wife – you know that'll never happen, don't you? In this house you'll have to take part in the communal life of the place. You'll have to support yourself. You might have to work.

**Changez**    I would do anything to be with you.

**Karim** (*to the audience*)    The three of us were bound together by ties stronger than personality, and stronger than the liking or disliking of each other.

I thought what a terrific person Jamila had become. There was in her a great depth of will, of delight in the world, and so much energy for love. Her feminism and sense of self seemed to illuminate her tonight as she went forward; an Indian woman, who would fight to live a useful life in white England.

*The phone rings in the phone box and* **Karim** *answers it. His dad is on the other end.*

**Haroon**    How's your mother, Karim? I can't stop worrying about her.

*Before* **Karim** *can answer,* **Eva** *grabs the phone.*

**Eva**    Goodbye, Karim!

*She slams it down and* **Haroon** *crumbles over in pain.*

**Haroon**    I feel like a criminal; someone living happily on money he's committed grievous bodily harm to obtain.

**Eva** (*crying out as if wounded*)    But you don't want her! You weren't right for each other! You were together long enough to know that!

**Haroon**    I could have done more. She didn't deserve to be hurt so. I don't believe in people leaving people.

**Eva**    But you still did it!

**Haroon**    Because you made me!

**Eva**    This guilt and regret will ruin us!

**Haroon**    It is part of me –

**Eva**    Please, please, clear it out of your mind. And out of my life.

**Haroon**    What if I can't?

**Jeeta** *enters with a saucepan and the fox reappears. She wafts the air so he smells the delicious scent.*

**Jeeta**    Ha! Greedy brother likes my Saag Aloo as well. You and I will change the world Mr Fox. Just you see.

*A drunk walks past and throws a beer can at the fox who runs away.*

**Drunk**    Fuck you, foxy.

**Jeeta** *hides and speaks to the stars.*

**Jeeta**    We will change the bloody world.

*She leaves, stirring her magic pot.*

*From the phone box,* **Karim** *dials the commune.* **Changez** *picks up.*

**Changez**    I love the communal life, Karim. The family atmosphere is here without nagging aunties. Except for the meetings, yaar. Still, it's bloody amazing and everything, the nudity you see daily.

**Karim**    Nudity?

**Changez**    Full nudity. Complete nudity. There are five girls here, and only Simon and I representing the gentlemen's side. And the girls, on the communist principle of having no shame to hide, go completely without clothes, their breasts without brassieres! Their bushes without concealment!

**Karim**    Christ –

**Changez**    But I can't stay there –

**Karim**    Why not, Bubble?

**Changez**    Karim, it breaks my heart, yaar. Jamila has started to yell with this nice boy, Simon. They are in the next room. Every night they blast my bloody ears to Kingdom Coming.

**Karim**    Why don't you change rooms?

**Changez**    I like to be near her. I like to hear her moving around. At this moment she is sitting down. At that moment she is reading. I like to know.

**Karim**    Love can be very much like stupidity.

**Changez**    Love is love, and it is eternal. You don't have romantic love in the West. You sing about it on the radio but no one really loves here.

**Karim**    What about Eva and Dad?

**Changez**    That's adultery. That's pure evil. I'm going out. I need some air. Love you.

*He puts down the phone and leaves the house. He is met by a gang. It is the National Front. One is the* **Drunk** *with a beer can. We see* **Changez** *followed, intimidated and brutally beaten.*

**Jamila** *runs to her phone in distress and dials.* **Karim** *answers from the phone box.*

**Jamila**    Creamy! Changez has been attacked – a gang jumped out on him. They planted their feet all over him and

carved the initials of the National Front into his stomach
with a razor blade.

**Karim**   Fuck. Is he ok?

**Jamila**   He's shocked, shit-scared and shaken up – but he's
alive.

**Karim**   Have you called the police?

**Jamila**   They suggested that he'd laid down under the
railway bridge and inflicted the wound on himself.

**Karim**   What can I do?

**Jamila**   Come and march with us. Trafalgar Square in an
hour. These attacks are happening all the time and we need
to make our voices heard.

**Karim**   I'll be there.

*He starts to leave but has another thought. He returns to the phone,
puts money in the slot and calls* **Eleanor**.

**Karim**   Eleanor. We've got to confront the fascists. There's a
march on. Will you come?

**Eleanor**   When?

**Karim**   Now.

**Eleanor**   Now? I'll have to think.

**Karim**   Please. Trafalgar Square. I'll pick you up and drop
you off. I really need you.

**Eleanor**   Alright. But don't come round. I'll see you there,
love. My head's a little messed up.

*She puts on her coat and leaves the house.*

**Jamila** (*shouting across London*)   Come on, Creamy! You'll
miss the demo.

**Karim** (*shouting back*)   I'll see you there.

*He sets off to join the march but thinks again. He turns round and finds himself outside* **Pyke**'s *door. When* **Eleanor** *comes out she sees* **Karim**.

**Eleanor**   What are you doing here?

**Karim**   I thought that you were going to throw your body at the fascists, not at Matthew.

**Eleanor**   Pyke's an exciting man.

**Karim**   How long's it been going on?

**Eleanor**   Since that time we went over there for supper and you and Pyke did that stuff to each other.

**Karim**   Will you carry on sleeping with him?

**Eleanor**   If he asks me. Yes.

*She rests her head against* **Karim**'s *chest.*

**Karim**   Oh, love –

**Eleanor**   I want you to be with me, Karim. But I can't have people – men – telling me what to do. If Pyke wants me to be with him, then I must follow my desire. There's so much for him to teach me. And please, please, don't ever follow me again.

**Karim** (*to the audience*)   It was over. My first real love affair. I had pursued my English rose as my dad had pursued England, as if by possessing these prizes, we stared defiantly into the eye of the Empire and all its self-regard.

*We hear the distant sound of applause.*

Even the cheers of the audience on Matthew Pyke's opening night couldn't fill the gap in my aching heart.

*He is swamped by cheering fans, including* **Margaret** *and* **Haroon** *who seem to be talking to each other and smiling. We are at the theatre after the opening night of* **Pyke**'s *play.* **Eva** *is the first to congratulate* **Karim**.

**Eva**   Karim, Karim, Karim! You were fabulous! The play was amazing, darling. It was about this country. About how callous and bereft of grace we've become. It made the hair on the back of my neck stand up. I judge all art by its effect on my neck.

**Karim**   I'm glad it did that, Eva.

*They both look at* **Haroon** *and* **Margaret**.

**Eva**   It's a happy sight, isn't it?

**Changez** *limps up. He is visibly injured, bandaged with his arm in a sling but his spirit is resolutely positive.*

**Eva**   Hello, Changez. Nice to see you up and about. How are you feeling?

**Changez**   Much better.

**Eva**   Everything healing nicely?

**Changez**   Top notch.

**Eva**   Terrible business, those bloody thugs.

**Changez** (*to* **Karim**)   Very good plays and top playing! Come a little closer, top actor, and listen to my criticism. I am glad you didn't try the leap of invention into my character. Good!

**Karim**   You look happy, Changez. What's brought on this ecstasy?

**Changez**   But surely you will have guessed, my Jamila is expecting. We are having a baby.

**Karim**   Your baby?

**Changez**   You bloody fool, how could that be without sexual intercourse? You know very well I haven't had the extent of that privilege.

**Karim**   That's what I thought.

**Changez**   So, by Simon she is expecting. But we will all share in it.

**Karim**   A communal baby?

**Changez**   Belonging to the entire family of friends. I've never been so happy.

**Karim** *calls to* **Jamila** *who glowers at him.*

**Karim**   Jammie! Jammie! Congratulations!

**Jamila** *scowls.*

**Karim**   What's your problem?

**Jamila**   You weren't there. I can't believe it. You just didn't show up.

**Karim**   Where wasn't I? Where?

**Jamila**   At the demonstration, Karim.

**Karim**   I couldn't make it, Jammie. I was rehearsing. How was it?

**Jamila**   Other people from the cast of your play were there. Right at the front. Where are you going as a person, Karim?

**Karim**   Over there.

*He goes to* **Margaret**, *who hugs and kisses him.*

**Margaret**   I love you so much

**Karim**   Wasn't I good, eh, Mum?

**Margaret**   Well, you weren't in a loincloth which is something. But, Karim, you're not an Indian. You've never been to India. You'd get diarrhoea the minute you stepped off that plane, I know you would.

**Karim**   Why don't you say it a bit louder, Mum? Anyway, aren't I part Indian?

**Margaret**   Who gave birth to you? You're an Englishman.

**Karim**    I don't care. I'm an actor.

**Margaret**    Don't say that. Be what you are.

*She looks across at* **Haroon**, *who is now with* **Eva**. **Eva** *is talking angrily to him.*

**Margaret**    She's giving him a thick ear. Silly old cow.

*She starts to cry.*

**Karim**    Go to the ladies and blow your nose.

**Margaret**    I better.

**Karim** (*to the audience*)    The play didn't last long in the West End, a month only. Before Eleanor went off to play a small part in the big film and Pyke flew off to San Francisco to teach, Matthew gathered us together after our final show.

**Pyke** *brings the company together for a group huddle and they all do a 'One for all and all for one!' As usual,* **Pyke** *holds court.*

**Pyke**    Time for the big reveal!

*He goes to the audience member from earlier and asks for his list back. He reads out the predictions he'd written down on the first day of rehearsals.*

(*Laughing smugly.*) Karim, you'll be riveted by this.

**Karim**    How do you know?

**Pyke**    I know.

'Karim is obviously looking for someone to fuck. Either a boy or a girl but he really doesn't mind. But he'd prefer a girl, because she will mother him. It'll be Eleanor. He thinks she's sweet, but she's not blown away by him. I'll have a word with her, tell her to take care of Karim, give him a bit of confidence. My prediction is that Eleanor will fuck him, it'll basically be a mercy fuck, but he'll fall hard for her and she'll be too kind to tell him the truth about anything. It will end in tears.'

**Karim** *screams. He throws himself across the bar and tries to destroy* **Pyke**. *There is a messy tangle; arms and legs everywhere.* **Karim** *is in a frenzy, kicking, scratching and screaming. He falls back and hits his head on a table. The world stops and a heavenly creature arrives.*

**Charlie**   Shhh, little one. I'm here now.

*He wraps* **Karim** *in a blanket, and kisses and smiles at him.*

**Charlie**   Welcome to my place. I know you feel like shit, but we're going to have fun like you've never known it. Now, let's start off as we intend to go on!

Move in. Move in tonight. I'm rich and famous now. I have everything you need. I'd love to have you with me.

*They snuggle close, smoke and listen to music.*

I remember when I fell in love for the first time. I was staying in a beautiful house in Santa Monica. It had five terraces on the side of a steep, lush hill and a huge swimming pool. I'd just been for a swim when the wife of the famous actor whose house it was came out and handed me the keys to her motorcycle. A Harley. It was then I knew what I loved. Money. Money and everything it could buy. I never wanted to be without money again because it could buy me the life I wanted.

**Karim**   Money is the best, Charlie. But if you're not careful it'll fertilise weirdness, indulgence and greed. Matthew has money and look what happened with him?

*He smokes.*

Money can cut the cord between you and ordinary living.

**Charlie**   I enjoy these conversations, Karim. I just thank God that I'm not pretentious like you.

**Karim**   Charlie, I'm so lonely. There are people around me, but all I see is Eleanor and I can't bear it. It's breaking my heart.

*He starts to weep. Uncontrollably. He is filled with self-hatred and a desire to sleep and hurt himself.* **Charlie** *takes care of him giving him money, holding him, handing him drinks and lighting cigarettes as he flails in despair. The fever passes and* **Karim** *picks up a paper. He sees the date.*

**Karim**    It's been six months, Charlie. I think it is time for me to go.

**Charlie**    Stay here with me where you belong, Karim. There's a lotta bastards out there. You got everything you need, haven't you?

**Karim**    Sure I have. It's just that I –

**Charlie**    Let's go shopping for clothes, ok? Or shall we just stay here and listen to some more music?

**Karim** (*to the audience*)    It was eerie, our growing dependency on each other. I suspected that he liked having me there as a witness. Only I could appreciate how far he'd come from his school days in Bromley. I was a mirror. I was a full-length mirror that could remember.

*A woman in black leather arrives carrying a holdall.*

**Charlie**    You want to join in? I'm going to the edge, man. I'm going to experience pain. The deep human love of pain. Come with me, Karim.

**Karim** (*to the audience*)    I remembered the night in Beckenham when I tried to kiss him and he turned his face away.

**Charlie**    Little one?

**Karim**    I'm moving out, Charlie. I've got an audition.

**Charlie**    You don't need an audition. I'll give you a salary. You'll be a little fat cat.

**Karim** (*to the audience*)    I remembered the night in the garden when I saw Dad screwing Eva – my introduction to betrayal, deceit and heart-following.

(*To* **Charlie**.) I don't think so, big one.

**Charlie**   What are you talking about? I'm going on a world tour. LA, Sydney, Toronto. I want you to be there with me. It's the high life. Just what we always dreamt of.

**Karim**   I'm leaving.

**Charlie**   You can't go.

**Karim**   Charlie.

**Charlie**   You won't like it. Please stay.

**Karim** (*to the audience*)   Tonight Charlie's face was open and warm. There was no rejection in it. I never thought he would look at me like this.

(*To* **Charlie**.) No, Charlie.

**Karim** *shakes his head. The woman produces a hood from the holdall. She pushes a handkerchief into* **Charlie**'s *mouth and slips the hood over his head.* **Charlie** *is gone.*

**Karim** *hears birdsong and starts to gently dance.*

**Pyke** *appears in his dressing gown.*

**Pyke**   Karim! Why don't you pop over for a drink.

**Karim**   Sorry, Matthew. I've got people to see.

*He goes to his childhood home.* **Margaret** *is shocked.*

**Karim**   Hi, Mum.

**Margaret**   What are you doing here? You can't come in. I have a friend coming round.

**Karim**   A friend?

**Margaret**   Shoo!

**Karim**   I won't shoo! Tell me all, Mum.

**Margaret**   Alright. I've been seeing someone. His name is Jimmy.

**Karim**   How's long's it been going on?

**Margaret**   Four months or so, since the divorce.

**Karim**   Where did you meet?

**Margaret**   Life-drawing class . . . Stop asking bloody questions, Karim. I'm not going to tell you any more about him because you're not allowed to meet him.

**Karim**   Why not?

**Margaret**   He doesn't know my exact age. He's seen pictures of you, but only ones where you were only ten or something. He might be shocked to discover I've got a son as old as you are. So shoo!

**Karim**   Good for you, Mum. You deserve it.

*He knocks on* **Eva**'s *door.*

**Eva**   Karim!

**Karim**   It's good to see you again, Eva. You've no idea how much I missed you.

**Eva**   Why are you talking so formally? Have you forgotten how to talk to your own family? Your dad will be so pleased to see you. (*She calls.*) Haroon! Look who's back!

**Haroon** *appears.*

**Haroon**   Hello, prodigal boy.

**Eva** *strokes* **Haroon**'s *cheek tenderly.*

**Eva**   Before I met your father, I had no courage and little faith. Now I am beginning to feel I can do anything. And so is he, aren't you, my darling? Karim, your father has news. Tell him!

**Haroon**   I'm leaving my job. I've given my notice. I'm going to teach and think and listen. I will encourage people to contemplate, to let go. I will help them contemplate the deeper wisdom of themselves, wisdom which is often concealed in the rush of everyday life. Oh, Karim, the years I've wasted. This is the meaning of my life. Good, eh?

**Karim**   It's the best thing I've heard you say, Dad.

**Eva** *leaves.*

**Karim**   Dad. Mum's seeing someone – a man.

**Haroon**   What kind of a man? Do you think he's kissing her?

**Karim**   I'm sure of it. She's better than I've seen her for years, good-tempered and optimistic and all.

**Haroon**   Good God. How can that possibly be? She was always the world's sweetest but most miserable woman. Nothing will ever be the same again.

**Karim**   How could it be?

**Pyke** *appears.*

**Pyke**   The champagne's on ice!

**Karim**   Still no, Matthew!

*He knocks on the door of Paradise Stores and* **Jeeta** *opens it. She looks beautiful in a smart apron and new clothes.*

**Jeeta**   Karim, my fire eater! You hungry?

**Karim**   Yes, Auntie!

**Jeeta**   I got everything for you, samosa, black dahl, chick pea dahl, green dahl, pigeon peas, tarka dahl. And kebabs.

**Karim**   Everything Auntie. How's life?

**Jeeta**   Very good! Very bloody, bastard, bollocks good! I own my own restaurant now. No husband, no shop, no daughter to weigh me down. Just me and my bloody, bastard, bollocks, brilliant, business brain. Oh! How the English love to murder an Indian . . .

**Karim** *knocks on the commune's door.* **Changez** *opens it. He hasn't fully recovered from the attack. He holds a baby in his arms.*

**Changez**   Shhh! This is the daughter of the house, Leila Kollontai, and she's asleep at last. Our baby. Top naughty.

**Karim**   Where is everyone?

**Changez**   Mr Simon the father is away in America. He's been long gone, lecturing on the history of the future. He's a big man.

**Karim**   And Jamila?

**Changez**   She's here, intact and all, upstairs. But she won't be happy to talk to you, no, no, no, no. She'll be happy to barbecue your balls and eat them with peas.

**Karim**   What are you talking about, Bubble?

**Changez**   You're still in the bloody shit, Karim. And what are you going to do about it? Jammie won't forgive you for not putting your face in it at the demonstration. That's the thing you should be worried about, yaar.

**Jamila** *appears*. **Joanna** *appears behind her.*

**Jamila**   Hallo, Karim

**Joanna**   I'm sure we've seen each other somewhere.

**Jamila**   He's a big famous actor. Aren't you, dear?

**Joanna**   That's it. I saw the play you were in. You were great in it. You liked it too, didn't you, Changez? You persuaded me to go and see it.

**Changez**   I don't think I liked it as much as I said, Joanna. What I remember of it has left little permanent trace in my memory. It was white people's thing, wasn't it, Jammie?

**Karim**   What do you do, Joanna?

**Joanna**   I'm a film-maker. Jamila and I are making a documentary together. Wouldn't it be great if there was grapefruit and toast for breakfast again.

**Changez**   Oh yes, Don't you worry, there will be, for you and Jamila at nine on the dot. I will bring it to your room.

**Jamila** *and* **Joanna** *leave.*

**Karim**   Wow. How d'you feel about all this?

**Changez**   Feel? All in this house are trying to love each other, Karim! It's simple to grasp. Jammie loves two people, that's all. She loves Simon, but he's not here. She loves Joanna, and Joanna is here.

**Changez** *pauses, distracted.*

**Karim**   What's the matter, Bubble?

**Changez**   You make me think about too many things.

*The phone box rings and* **Karim** *goes to answer it.*

**Karim**   That's amazing. Thank you. Thank you. Yes! Absolutely. Yes.

*He punches the air in celebration and shouts out to all.*

Everyone. Come on! I'm taking you all to dinner. Have anything you like. It's all on me. D'you want dessert, d'you want coffee?

**Pyke** *arrives and puts his arm proprietorially around* **Karim**.

**Pyke**   What are we celebrating, gang? I'll have a glass of bubbly if you're asking.

**Karim**   No, Matthew, I'm not. It's friends and family only tonight.

**Pyke**   But I thought –

**Karim**   You thought wrong. Sorry, Matthew.

*He waves as* **Pyke** *leaves through the auditorium.*

**Haroon**   What is this all in aid of son? What's the bloody occasion?

**Karim**    I've got a job. I'm in a soap opera. (*In an Indian accent.*) Top pay. Top job. Top person.

**Haroon**    What is so funny about being Indian? Don't laugh in my face like an I'm idiot.

**Karim**    But I'm not. I wasn't.

**Margaret**    Well done love. We're really proud of you, too. Jimmy! Karim's got a new job!

**Jimmy**    Well done, Karim!

**Karim** (*to the audience*)    Maybe you never stop feeling like an eight-year-old in front of your parents.

**Eva**    Can I have some quiet for a few minutes? I also have an announcement.

**Haroon**    For God's sake make it, then.

**Eva**    Is it still true?

**Haroon**    It's true Eva.

**Karim**    Just say it, Eva, everyone's waiting.

**All**    Say it, say it!

**Eva**    All right. Pull yourself together, Eva. We are getting married.

*The friends and family gasp.*

Yes, we're getting married.

*The friends and family 'ah'.*

We met, fell in love, we're sorry and now we're getting married.

*The friends and family whoop and applaud.*

Please don't make me do this alone, Haroon. Say something.

**All**    Speech, speech!

**Haroon**    Ok. Ok. This woman, this generous, vivid and patient woman has changed my life. She has led me to myself and shown me colours I didn't know existed. Thank you, friends. Thank you, family. And thank you, Eva.

**Eva**    Oh, Haroon. My darling man . . .

*They kiss.*

In two months' time. Ok? You're all invited.

*The big, messy family roars its approval. They start to dance as they did at the beginning.*

**Karim**    And so I sat in the centre of this city that I loved, which itself sat at the bottom of a tiny island. I was surrounded by people I loved and the memories of those I had lost. I thought of Uncle Anwar fizzling out in an NHS hospital and of Charlie dying alone in a New York hotel. Who knew that you could feel so happy and so miserable at the same time? I thought about my new role – the rebellious son of an Indian shopkeeper in a soap opera. Not exactly changing the world but at least I didn't have to wear a yellow loincloth.

**Haroon** *hugs* **Karim.**

**Haroon**    You know I am so very proud of you, my boy. I love you.

**Karim**    I love you too, Dad.

**Haroon** *dances away.* **Karim** *closes his eyes.*

**Karim**    There was once a young man who was born and bred in a South London suburb. It was said of this suburb that when people drowned, they saw not their lives but their double-glazing flash before them.

He thought that life would be filled with spit-drenched woodwork cupboards and pissed-on shoes – until he discovered theatre and all the magic, melancholy and mess that tends to come with this most ancient of professions.

*He opens his eyes and smiles.*

What a mess everything's been. What a painful, cruel mess. But that it won't always be that way. It won't. Promise.

*The End.*